The White Pocketbook

Walter W. Bannon

Valerie,
Thanks,
8-24-13

DEDICATION

After writing the accounts of this book, I am compelled to dedicate it to the amazing men and women who fought and died in World War II. To those who survived and lived to tell about it, like Mom, and those who didn't, I also dedicate this story.

CONTENTS

Author Foreword

Preface   Pg 3

Introduction   Pg 5

1   Conversations   Pg 14

2   A Walloon Girl   Pg 25

3   The Invasion   Pg 36

4   Defiant Eyes   Pg 48

5   Unexpected Guest   Pg 58

6   Degrelle's Revenge Pg 70

7   Hitler's Anger   Pg 81

8   Life With The Allies Pg 95

9   My America   Pg 110

10 The American Hero   Pg 129

11 Growing Up Frenchie Pg 140

12 Bannon Family Singers Pg 156

13 Lessons Learned   Pg 167

14 Closing The Pocketbook Pg 175

Author Foreword

We are fortunate to have had such an accurate record of Andree's war experiences saved. Thousands of pictures and myriads of notes were reviewed to assemble this amazing account of her life during World War II. From the first events of the Nazi invasion of Belgium when she was only fourteen years old and forced to live in her basement for four years, to her transformation to an American wife, Andree's story takes you along on her emotional journey. Her struggle to survive the ruthless occupation is revealed in the heartbreaking collection of conversations between her and me. Her strength and character formed by her devastating circumstances are an ever-present testament to her spirit.

Preface

Sometimes a voice emerges from the most unlikely of places, a voice that changes the way you see life and the people all around you. You hear about tragic events and you ask yourself how this could happen over and over, but you get no satisfaction after searching the deepest corners of your mind. Finally, you have no recourse but to land all of your wanderings at the doorstep of insanity, or worse yet, evil.

Very few words have torn into my heart and left an imprint the way Mom's did the day she said to me, "They ruined my life!"

Her eyes melted with anguish, and she sat motionless with her head tilted downward in an almost remorseful pose. The silence seemed like an eternity following that mournful comment. Stunned, and taken by surprise by her confession, I stood there broken in spirit. Then, timidly and gently, I asked her, "Who did, Mom?"

I had always looked at my mother as a pillar of strength. She had it all together. I knew she had been through tough times during World War II, but I'd always thought that she'd felt her life was part of a divine plan. I had never heard her say a negative thing about her life all during my childhood. Was she still bitter? I wondered. Were there scars that had not healed from holding the memories of war locked inside her heart for so many years?

I hoped to get the story out someday but I never knew quite how that would come about. Time was running short for me to ever find out what happened in Belgium when Nazi troops poured into her quiet village. Mom's day-to-day recollections were beginning to separate into pieces, and the pendulum of time was seemingly ticking faster and faster with every year that passed. I worried that she might end up being one of those unfortunate ones whose stories remained untold. In referring to Anne Frank, Primo Levi writes, "One single Anne Frank moves us more than the countless others who suffered just as much as she did, but whose faces have remained in the shadows (Levi)." It was time to bring Mom's story out of the shadows.

INTRODUCTION

It was a beautiful day for a wedding. Danny and Mylan, my son and his fiancée, would be married at two pm. The setting in the picturesque village in western Maine couldn't have been more perfect for the myriad of pictures being taken against the backdrop of Long Lake and from the lawn of the historic chapel sitting guard quietly over the causeway on Route 302 in Naples. After the ceremony, the wedding party lined up at the water's edge on the pier, for group photos, while in the background swimmers and boats faded in and out of the scenes. We watched with joy to see my son, Andree's grandson, carefully hold his lovely new bride adorned in white while surrounded by a sea of yellow bridesmaid's dresses. "Don't fall in," we jokingly yelled out to the bride and groom. Mom glared at me with warning eyes when I came back to the reception and told her about it. She didn't think it was wise to do anything on the edge.

Mom was always the cautious one. She didn't care to push the margins of safety at this point in her life. It was a comfortable place for her to walk, now that she had raised six children and was seeing her grandkids growing up. She had tiptoed through the minefields of war-torn Europe and had maneuvered the paths to the American dream by walking the centerline of security. Mom was now as wise as an owl and as cautious as an eagle, seemingly able to spot danger from a great distance.

As for relationships, she had the same protocol. She often told me that she didn't always trust people that she met, at first. Mom said that it was because of the war. Everyone was on her list of potential enemies until time and familiarity would erase those suspicions. When I would introduce her to a new friend, she would ask me a dozen questions about the friend before she felt comfortable. It was ten times more difficult for Mom to accept new acquaintances if their names were Germanic.

Mom's challenges were not only social. She had language barriers that often left us in stitches. One day when my daughter, Amanda, introduced her fiancé to Grandma Andree, Mom smiled and asked him if she could give him a "French kiss." Now in Belgium that means a kiss is given on each cheek, but in America it's quite different. Shaun drew back in surprise at the thought of making out with his future grandmother-in-law.

The day following the wedding, Mom and my two older sisters, Marian and Elaine, with their husbands, John and Dave, had settled into their hotel in New Hampshire, just a short drive from Naples. Interestingly, the hotel they stayed at looks a lot like an old European village home. This hotel, called The Stonehurst Manor, sits high on a hill in North Conway and looks out over Mount Washington, the highest peak in the Northeast. Mount Washington is often snow-capped in the summer time and, in so many ways, reminds me of the mountains in southern France and Belgium. Perhaps this similarity is why they often chose to stay there. It would, in a way, be so much like the Belgian village that Mom grew up in.

When I was stationed in Germany for two years while I served in the United States Army, I had several opportunities to travel around Europe on rail-pass train tickets. At the end of my two years, I took thirty days of accumulated vacation time to see as much of Europe as I could. For about two hundred dollars, I managed to travel from Germany to Belgium, England to Spain, then on to France and Monaco, briefly touching into Italy, before returning to Germany. I had a backpack with a sleeping bag and, as often as I could, slept for free at youth hostels.

Crossing the English Channel on an air-powered Hovercraft and landing at the White Cliffs of Dover was an experience I'll never forget. The ride was like skiing down a mountain of moguls as the Hovercraft, riding on a cushion of air, rose and fell between the large ocean swells. On the return trip from England, I was in an overcrowded ferry at night. In the standing room only ship, I felt claustrophobic. To add to my upset stomach, I then heard a man yelling, "She's going down!" I began to worry about our safety and asked the gentleman next to me why everyone wasn't getting to the lifeboats. He calmly replied, "Oh, he always does that, he's just drunk!"

Being an American soldier provided me with several opportunities to visit Switzerland, Austria, and France. I once stayed at a beautiful resort in Berchtesgaden, Germany, called "The Berghoff." This resort used to be one of Hitler's hideaways. He and Eva Braun, his future bride, spent many days at this remarkable spot with a stunning vista of the snow-capped mountains. I also visited the Swiss Alps, learning to ski by going to the peak of one of those huge mountains with a few of my army friends. They assured me that all I needed to do to ski was to point my skis downhill, and when I wanted to stop; I just had to cross the tips. Well, my first trip down that huge mountain took about an hour. I fell every fifty feet. I would not suggest to anyone who wants to learn to ski to go to the top of a Swiss mountain. I remember thinking that the ski lift had no end as it ascended up and up, until everything at the base was gone from sight. I was so scared, and I knew that there was only one way home.

I also visited Mozart's home in Austria, and looked out his music room window to see the unbelievably beautiful mountain landscape. The white peaks jutted so high, then instantly collapsed into river gorges thousands of feet below. I still remember thinking about how inspired Mozart must have been to see that scene everyday. Perhaps this scene is what inspired so many European composers to create their musical masterpieces.

I learned to kayak on an icy cold river that flowed between Austria and Switzerland. The sights were not the only breathtaking experience on these trips. The cold water took my breath away when I had to practice a full rollover in the kayak. I loved the kayaking but dreaded having to practice those rollovers.

Back at the manor in New Hampshire, Mom sat in front of the grand fireplace reading a book she'd found on the shelf of the hotel's library. She was always well rested and ready to go to at least an hour before everyone else. By nine o' clock, the rest of the group was ready for a little excursion through North Conway in hopes of finding a quaint breakfast nook, so they headed out together. Their searching didn't take long, as they pulled into an informal restaurant offering a budget meal. Andree, Marian, Elaine, John, and Dave headed for a table at the back of the room. The setting was in a sunken-floored section. This gave the room a slight look of separation from the rest of the establishment. "What a fantastic trip," Mom said, as she recalled the wedding events of Saturday.

Everything was perfect. It was sunny and warm outside, so after eating, they planned to drive around the area to take in the lovely scenes, along with the skyline views of the White Mountains.

"Are we ready?" Marian asked. When the girls and their spouses all got up to leave, Mom wrapped her sweater around her and headed out following the group. As she stepped up to cross the threshold of the sunken room, she didn't quite maneuver her footsteps correctly. Her balance became unstable and, in a colossal way, Mom went crashing down into the table of patrons next to her, spilling their meals and making quite the scene. She had fallen in grand fashion and now lay there on the floor, helpless. She apologized profusely to the diners, and they were very accepting. But now, for the first time in her life, she realized that she couldn't move. She had experienced being frozen from fear when a German soldier once held a gun to her head. She also knew what it was like to be detained in her own home. She knew the heartbreak of being interred for being suspected of being a spy, but this was a totally different experience.

Dave, being a six-foot-two-inch tall high school coach, picked up her eighty-pound fragile frame in both arms and brought her to the car. She was in severe pain, and by the looks of things, had broken something in her hip area. She winced in pain unable to hide how much it hurt. As tears rolled from her eyes, Mom was quickly transported to the emergency room at North Conway's Memorial Hospital just a short ride away.

The doctors told us that evening, after being x-rayed, that she had multiple breaks and would be in the hospital for at least a week, after which, she would be in a local rehabilitation facility for another month or two. Although this was tragic and frustrating for her, I began to see it as the opportunity that, for so long, I had hoped for. She would be stuck in Maine for many weeks during her recovery and I would finally get a chance to ask her about her life in Belgium. This moment in her life was perhaps one of her darkest times but, looking past the pain, it would turn into one of the most important moments in both of our lives.

I spoke with all of my family members about getting her life story recorded. They all agreed that it was important for us to use this opportunity, with Mom in her golden years, to open the vault of her life and allow her to finally share with her children all of the hidden treasures of her heart.

1. CONVERSATIONS

I sat on the edge of Mom's bed at the Memorial Hospital and asked her how she was doing. She was obviously very distraught and asked, "How could God do this to me?"

The ever-strong mother I had always turned to for answers when I needed them was now asking me a very simple, yet complicated question. It was troubling for me to hear her talk that way. In times like these it's so simple to quote phrases or scripture verses to respond to life's tough challenges, but this was different. This was Mom, and a short response that didn't come from the heart was simply pouring gas on the fire. She would see right through any simple insincere response that I might conjure up. I needed something more than words. I needed something honest and something real to give her.

"Everything is going to be okay," I said as I squeezed her hand in mine. It may have been a weak response, but it was a response that came from my heart. After that I said, "We have to look for the good that can come out of difficult times." I have to admit that it felt kind of rewarding to be on this side of the advice-giving fence for the first time in my life with Mom.

In truth, I was very concerned about reports I had heard recently concerning elderly patients who had broken their hips. The reports I read showed statistics of patients who've had shortened lives after these types of accidents. Some reports that I read told of people who lived only a year or two following hip surgery. I thought about all of the possibilities and the idea that this could be the case with Mom. It gave me pause to think about her life story, and how we might learn more of what she went through during World War II while she waited out her healing. I didn't tell her about the statistics that I had learned about.

As we visited Mom in her hospital room, on occasion she would leak out a line or two about a situation from life in

Belgium that challenged her in a similar way. She would talk about the food in the hospital being inedible at times. She had particular things that she would eat and, if the menu wasn't to her liking, she would just not eat. It was perhaps then, sitting there in the most awkward place in her life that she spoke the words that triggered my resolve to probe into her memory for the truth. I said that she needed to eat her food for strength. I asked her if she was hungry, and she answered tersely, "I am never hungry!"

This wasn't a typical response. It was a very unusual thing to say. It sounded to me like a learned response from a childhood trauma being relived. I needed more explanation about why she would ever say that. "What do you mean, Mom? Of course, you must be hungry," I responded.

She said again, "I am never hungry. I survived the war when we had no food, didn't I?"

"Then, what did you do? Everyone has to eat," I said.

"No. My father knew a man who had a farm, and sometimes we could get an egg or two, and once in a while, a chicken. We could mix that with grass and eat grass soup.

There were also small gardens that sometimes we could get some vegetables from, but I got used to not eating when there was no food. So, I have disciplined myself, and now I can say I am never hungry!"

Now being in a land where food is never lacking, I found it almost childish to not eat and to revert to a place in her life of almost seventy years ago. At only eighty pounds, Mom needed to be eating. Although it frustrated me to hear her say this, it began to open a window of understanding and an acceptance of who she was. I began to see Mom as more of the survivor than the pillar of strength I always knew. Her words were just showing me how all of those experiences that she had as a little girl formed her into who she was today. Mom was sitting in front of me, not as mother, but as the product of a society that was torn into shreds by the tragedy of war. I was standing in the presence of a survivor. Not just any survivor, but one who held a library of experiences inside her mind that the family had yet to learn the entirety of.

Looking back at the things she would feed us when we were young allowed me to piece together the reasons all six of her children grew up so thin. I remember Mom sometimes being embarrassed to see so much food being served in a restaurant. I know that being abundantly blessed at certain times caused her to feel guilty. The full refrigerators in America were nothing like the ones in Belgium. I believe everything she did was balanced against the backdrop of her youth, when they often managed without the basic necessities of life, including food.

One Thanksgiving when I was only about ten years old, our family had very little to eat. Somehow word spread to the small community of Noank, Connecticut, where we grew up, that the Bannon family needed some help. Mom had been cleaning houses for extra money, and Dad was away on one of his worldwide Army recruiting jobs. With six kids, times were often tough. However, I think Mom was okay with this challenge. When the grocery store delivered a box of food and a turkey to our doorstep, Mom told the deliveryman to take it back. He did as he was told, but when the storeowner found out what she had done, he personally came to our house and demanded that she accept the gift. Eventually, Mom gave in. For this special day, she lowered her proud stance as a self-sufficient war survivor and relented, allowing this act of kindness to go on, but just this once.

In another more comical instance, Mom, not being very aware of how American companies package and advertise on their cans of food products, accidentally sent my older brother, Chris, off to Noank Elementary School with his tuna fish sandwich made and his lunchbox packed with goodies. When he ate his meal, he was somewhat disgusted with the taste of his sandwich, but we didn't really have much room to complain about our food around Mom. Chris finished his meal, but when he returned home from school, he told her how bad the tuna fish sandwich tasted. Surprised at this, they retrieved the opened can from the trash to check the expiration date. They discovered, after carefully reading the label together, that she had made his sandwich with a perfectly fine can of tuna fish flavored cat food!

Mom had a tough time transitioning from her Belgian culture to America. She once made my dad spaghetti dinner using tomato catsup as sauce. Spaghetti was his favorite meal, but she would never eat it. She said it tasted like rubber and that it once made her terribly sick. After that meal, Dad would usually go out to eat at a restaurant if he wanted a good Italian dinner.

I keenly remember having to hide in my pockets the disgusting canned corn and peas she so often fed us, to make

Mom think I had eaten my food. We were never allowed to leave the dinner table unless our plates were clean. Together, all six children sat lined up three per side at our old bullet scarred dinner table, eating our meals out of brown Army issue bowls. I was sixteen when I ate my first corn on the cob. Mom said it was not typical to have this at a dinner table in Belgium. She said that corn on the cob was served to the pigs.

As fate would have it, with Mom now in her incapacitated situation, I had the fortune to have many conversations with her. Sometimes we would be sitting together eating dinner and it would hit me like a rock, "Do you realize who you are sitting next to?" This frail woman actually lived the things we only read about in history books. The Battle of the Bulge pushed through her village. She lived every bit of it. She had friends killed, she saw Jewish neighbors being rounded up and taken to labor camps, she experienced betrayals by her best friends, and even had her home bombed out, requiring her to live in their villa's basement for four years. It was just starting to sink in, how amazing her life experiences were.

Once Mom was well enough to leave the hospital, she would still need two months of therapy to regain her strength enough to walk, so it was decided that we would have her stay with us at our home in Bridgton, Maine. An author friend was willing to help record her recollections, and Mom agreed to be interviewed by her regularly so that we could collect her memoirs. I also began to write down in a booklet every event that I was hearing about for the first time.

Mom seemed willing to let out these painful events in pieces. Sometimes our conversations would get to be too much, and I would stop asking her questions. It was as though she was willing to open the vault of her memory, but only for short intervals, so that she could rest her mind from the difficulty of reliving the experiences for me. Every time I learned something new about her, it went into my notes.

On one evening at home, I thought it might be interesting for us to watch a World War II movie about submarines. She always got excited about seeing American army tanks and men in military uniforms, so I plugged in the movie. It seemed she was enjoying the opening, but as soon as she heard the German language being spoken, she left the room and sat alone upstairs, obviously very upset. Out of respect for her, I shut off the movie. I think it was just too difficult for her to hear the language of the German soldiers again, even after seventy years. Dr. Dobson writes that, when we are young, our emotions are so intense that any wounds and injuries we receive may stay with us for a lifetime (Dobson).

So it was, day in and day out, that I learned how to talk with Mom. At times, she would get red faced, and at other times, she would get tears in her eyes. Some conversations drew out her anger and others her pain. I was beginning to understand a little about the past experiences that molded young Andree Florin into who she is today.

Mom returned to Stonington, Connecticut, after her rehabilitation was complete. As fate would have it however, she would return to Maine almost a year later along with a U-Haul truck filled to capacity with her lifelong collection of memories. Mom's next year would add to those memories as she became immersed in life as a Mainer. Our basement was now filled with dozens of boxes that were jam packed with papers and personal items. I couldn't comprehend why she had so many boxes. What could she possibly have that was so important in all these packages full of paper, I wondered? She even brought her piano to Maine.

Mom loved the summer in Maine but hated the winter. The Maine winter reminded her of the coldest, snowiest winter she had ever seen in Belgium. It happened during the Battle of the Bulge when American and German troops became bogged down in deep snow and bitter cold in one of the worst storms in their history. Winters in Maine almost every year are similar to Belgium's worst. In Maine the snowfall is often measured in feet, not in inches like Mom was used to in Connecticut. Nonetheless, Mom completed her memoirs, and additionally I have garnered what I believe is a more complete picture of her life. I realize now that everything she did and said was in the context of what she lived through. From statements like "I am never hungry" to others like "They ruined my life," I began to understand her and why she didn't divulge her experiences voluntarily.

The more I learned, the more I had to humble myself to approach her with questions. Mom was a living memorial of an ocean of pain and unforgivable crimes. I often had to separate myself from her to take time alone to cry. In a small way, I was experiencing what she went through and it was breaking my heart into pieces.

On one quiet afternoon, I asked Mom if we could go through some of the boxes and perhaps weed out some of the things that she didn't need to hang onto anymore. It was during this joint effort of cleaning out old stuff that she removed an old, stained, white pocketbook with twin gold snaps. She held it near her heart for a moment until I asked her if we should throw it out. Mom first glared at me with piercing eyes, and then she smiled and replied, "This was the pocketbook I had when I was a little girl. When the war began, it was in my room. When our house was bombed everything was lost, but years after the war, a gentleman who bought the home was rebuilding it and he found my pocketbook. He located me and returned it to me." With a tear in my eyes and a gleam in hers, we opened it together.

2. A WALLOON GIRL

Belgian society at present is split into two main sects or groups of associations. The influences from France, Germany, and the Netherlands, all played important roles in creating modern day Belgium. This explains why Mom looked at me like I had sworn at her when I suggested that she was a Flemish girl. "I am not Flemish," Mom said.

I was somewhat shocked at her insistence that I get this right. She was from southern Belgium and that area is considered Walloon. The Walloon people speak their own romantic French language and, historically, are quite different. I guess that suggesting there is no big difference between Walloon and the northern Flemish was interpreted as an insult when so much pride had been placed on Mom's heritage. Flemish Belgians and Walloon Belgians are truly so different, culturally, that they could almost be considered as being from two different countries. Mom has reminded me several times that Bouillon, located in the heart of the Ardennes, is an important town and the residents are very proud of their significance during the early crusades and throughout history.

At fourteen years of age, a young and innocent little Walloon girl should have been spending her time chasing butterflies in a grassy meadow or dreaming about the day she'll walk the aisle in a flowing white gown with friends cheering, mothers crying, and fathers publicly stoic but actually crying on the inside. With so much to dream about, these years should have been a time when Andree would morph from adolescence into a young lady without the weight of the world on her shoulders. In Belgium in the 1930s, most of her young girlfriends imagined their futures and mused about which local boys would make good husbands. Many had already talked about what they wanted to be when they grew up, and most kept diaries that recorded who they'd expected they would marry. Some even tried to guess the age at which they would marry and who would join them in their wedding ceremonies as bridesmaids and flower girls.

Andree's dreams were no different. She penned her ideals on note papers. One read, "As a great granddaughter of the Duke, I will marry a rich man and live by the castle in a home looking down to the village." Every chance she'd get after arriving home from school, she would take her notes, fold them, and insert them into the white pocketbook that she received as a gift when she was only ten years old. She would also remove the black and white pictures she had collected and stare at them for a while. These photos included a few relatives, cousins, and friends. Perhaps she dreamed one of them could be someone she would fall in love with someday? Finally, she would snap shut its twin gold clips and place the pocketbook safely back on the shelf above her bed frame. In a way, this served as Andree's secret hope chest. Her future was secure within the twin gold snaps of that purse.

All of the girls born in the village of Bouillon were called "Great-granddaughters of the Duke." Duke Godfroi was the young, brave king most famous for giving his life in the quest to free Jerusalem from Muslim occupation in the first Christian crusade launched in 1095. In 1099, Godfroi, also a Walloon, succeeded in reclaiming Jerusalem. He was awarded the title of "Protector of the Holy Sepulcher." Godfroi was offered the title of "King of Jerusalem," but he refused it feeling that this title should only be bestowed on Christ (encyclopedia). Godfroi is known as the most Christian of all knights.

Godfroi's castle was built around 1070 and stands proud today over the town of Bouillon. His image is displayed in many of the Belgian households and, Godfroi's memorial statue of knighthood gallantry stands tall outside of the castle walls. Day after day, Andree would admire his courageous profile. She became immersed in awe from pictures and books she'd read about his life. "The man who marries me would need to be as important as this man was," Andree thought. She spent days on end just walking the castle walls, picking white flowers and dreaming about heroes, life to come, and who her knight in shining armor might be.

Andree's father, Auguste Felix Florin, born in Bouillon in 1902, was a well to do man with a well-established business in tobacco. He was not just selling tobacco, but he knew the best fields available and bought only the best of the leaves to assure a top quality product. The tobacco business was a strong thriving business in Europe, and Auguste Florin was very successful in making money at it. He kept the family on the path to success with the business handed down from Andree's grandfather, Auguste Florin, who had been born in Holland. Some advertising posters I found in Mom's papers date the beginning of this tobacco business to 1897.

Auguste Felix was also a man of integrity on whom the community could rely. All of the villagers knew and trusted him. He was always willing to consider the needs of the poor in the community. He was also a very kind and religious man who practiced his Catholic faith as well as he could. Mom used to tell me that her father had very special insights. Some might call it extra sensory perception, others a divine connection, but either way, she insisted he was always very aware of situations, dangers, and circumstances around him.

Andree's mother, Elizabeth Massina Florin, born in Cour Cheverr, France, also in 1902, was of Spanish descent and was a scientist until marrying Auguste. After marriage, she opened a jewelry shop in the center of Bouillon. Andree's parents' successes helped to provide a good home for Mom and her siblings Pierre, Dominic, and Monique. Mom was the second child born to Auguste and Elizabeth Florin.

Andree was born on August 3rd, 1926, in the quiet Walloon town of Bouillon, surrounded by the river Semois. The river loops through and around the village acting like a natural moat around the castle up on top of the hill. It then continues down to France running through the forest of the Ardennes, eventually meeting the Meuse River. The charm of this castle surrounded by white flowers, perched atop Bouillon's highest point, provided the perfect setting for magical dreams and heroes.

Mom attended the only school in the town. It was a Catholic school. From the ages of five to eleven, she would be taught academics by a bevy of strict nuns. Every day after lunch she would walk home and spend the afternoon playing outside their village home. The nuns had particular methods of securing their pupils' attention and respect. It was not uncommon for them to have a student hold out a hand to receive a whack from a ruler for misbehaving. The students' dinner manners were impeccable. If a child was to place her arms on the table during a meal, she would promptly be poked in the elbows with the tines of a dinner fork. Mom continued this particular discipline with all of her children at our dining table too.

I recall Mom telling me that the nuns would make her clean the rooms to perfection. They were not about foolishness or improper jesting. They were a very serious group.

When Mom turned twelve years old, she lived full time at a private girls' school called Soeur De Notre Dame. Dinners were typically vegetables and chicken. Dessert was only allowed on Sundays. Sometimes the nuns would bring them to a restaurant to eat and practice their dining skills in public. There a dessert called BaBa A Ruhm was served. It was a small cake soaked in liquor and topped with whipped cream. It was the best ever, and all of the young ladies loved it.

When she turned fourteen, Auguste hired a Belgian painter to capture the family he had raised in Bouillon. Albert Raty, born in 1889, also in Bouillon, was his first choice of artists. Raty was found to be deaf at the age of five. His family sent him off to attend an art school in Brussels, where his work was quickly recognized as unique. His thorough training soon opened doors for him in Paris at the Grande Chaumiere (Douffet). His works have become well known and are displayed at many museums and galleries. His paintings, like so many other French artists, are now very collectable.

Albert painted a solo portrait of Andree that shows the beauty she possessed as a young girl. Why Auguste hurried to get her portrait painted is unknown. Maybe he was concerned about how the war might end and whether or not his daughter would survive the coming rampage. Perhaps Auguste wanted to make sure he had something priceless to remember his family? It curiously shows her looking away, maybe in respect for the famous artist. Mom says that she remembers that he was deaf.

Andree attended Ste. Chretienne boarding school unsure about why she was sent there. Her mom said it was because they wanted her to have a better education, but it was also about this time that Hitler was beginning his invasion of the surrounding areas. Poland had just been invaded, and now looking west, Belgium, the Netherlands, and France were directly in the path of the Nazi war machine. Things were beginning to change around Bouillon, and, perhaps,

Auguste wanted to move Andree further away from any impending danger.

One scary event for the Florin family was when their Jewish friend's store was vandalized. The friend was a part of the close-knit business group that made up the downtown storefronts along the river's edge. Mom wondered why anyone would commit this crime against such a nice man. In Poland, not long before this occurred, Hitler's propaganda campaign to blame all Jews for the killing of a Nazi leader in France sparked a backlash that caused many Jewish businesses to be destroyed. On one horribly violent night now known as Kristallnacht, translated Night of the Broken Glass, it is recorded that seven thousand businesses were damaged or destroyed. History also records that thirty thousand Jews were taken to concentration camps following this rampage (ushmm.org). Other stories Auguste heard about local Jews being taken away to labor camps were very troubling.

The Florins had many close relationships in the village. One was with the family of Monsieur Degrelle. Mom knew them personally. She would go to their drug store to get medication for the family when it was needed. There were two brothers. One son, Leon Degrelle, was a Catholic man who had his own ideas of mixing Catholicism with a social engineering plan similar to socialism. This didn't sit well with Auguste, but he understood that everyone had different opinions about the war, so he allowed Leon this fantasy within their friendship. The other son, Edward Degrelle, was a pharmacist following in his father's profession. They were a Walloon family whose reputation would eventually rival that of Godfroi De Bouillon, Mom's beloved Duke.

In 1940, Andree lived away at school, but not away from the rising fear. While the shadows of the armies had not yet reached her home, the signs of an impending chaos were becoming evident. Soon, it wouldn't matter how much Auguste tried to surround his daughter with protection and shielding. The turmoil in France would quickly spill into Belgium and, like a tidal wave, destroy everything within its path.

3. THE INVASION

Life as she knew it with all of her dreams and plans was changing now for Andree. All of the schools were closed because of the war and she returned to live at home. She was only sixteen years old and this was her last involvement with schooling. There would be no graduation, no college, and no diploma. Life was not going according to plan. All of the treasured notes that she neatly tucked into her pocketbook over those precious early years of her life were suddenly looking like fool's gold.

Auguste, seeing the trouble approaching Belgium, took the entire family to France hoping to escape the approaching storm. They stayed with relatives believing there would be safety, but France soon became overrun with Nazi forces and the family was advised to make their way back to Belgium. Routes through the thick forest of the bordering Ardennes made it possible for Auguste to secretly cross the border at night. He also had a few connections along the way, which helped to secure a safe passage for the whole family.

Auguste knew the corridors of the Ardennes as well as anyone in Bouillon. The forest was dark and contained many dangers, including wild boar. Wild boars are very dangerous animals, especially when they feel threatened by humans. The wild boar is often seen in pictures when referring to the Ardennes forest.

On one afternoon, Auguste was told by his brother, Andree's Uncle Grusselin, a resistance fighter, that an Allied airplane had crashed somewhere in the forest. Feeling sure that they could find the site quickly, Auguste, Andree, and several other villagers headed out to see if the pilot might have survived the crash. They knew that it wouldn't be long before Nazi forces would realize the plane had crash landed in Bouillon and they'd be searching for it.

It didn't take long to spot the plane in a small clearing with the pilot standing nearby. Auguste ran up to him and explained that he would get him to safety in Bouillon. After a couple quick photographs with Andree sitting on top of the plane next to the pilot, the group headed back to the village where the pilot was hidden until he was passed safely back to his unit.

After Andree witnessed this event, she was charged by her father to always keep it a secret and to never share her secrets with anyone. She promised to keep what she had seen locked inside her memory forever. Auguste trusted Andree to keep her promise.

After Hitler's forces swept through Poland, they turned their attention west. France would be first. Hitler's forces invaded and occupied France in 1940. Now the Nazi armies were focused on both the western and eastern fronts. King Leopold's position of neutrality did little to slow down the *Blitzkrieg* or lightning attacks that Hitler's armies now employed. Belgium and Luxemburg were taken without much resistance, being small neutral countries with small armies.

Some Belgium residents had been secretly forming an underground communications network with other secret allied resistance members in France. They were called *Maquis*. The Maquis were reporting on German troop movements and were helping to disrupt their supply lines. Any of these activities, of course, if found out by the Germans, would immediately get one shot. All that the Nazi's needed was a suspicion that someone was involved with the resistance to receive the punishment of death by a bullet to the head. There was no court system now to give those accused of working against the Fuehrer a fair trial.

Auguste was part of this operation. Mom had some understanding that he was helping resist the invaders, but it was all superficial. It was known by the Nazis that there were messages being sent from the Belgian underground movement to the Allied members, and this infuriated the Nazi soldiers.

Now living at home, fear gripped Andree as she began to hear about atrocities being committed by the occupying German soldiers. Her dad was always in the basement doing something private, and her mom was trying to make life look normal, but Andree didn't like the new norms. If a German soldier was approaching the house, two taps on the floor warned Auguste that he needed to put everything away that he was working on in the basement and come upstairs.

One of those seemingly quiet afternoons, Auguste ran upstairs and said, "We must get Andree out of Belgium now." He had found out on his secret radio that the Germans were taking sixteen year old girls away to serve the German soldiers. He made arrangements to get her out of Belgium and to hide her in France. Auguste had some political connections in Rethel who would take her in until the danger had passed.

That night, under the secrecy of darkness, Auguste took Andree through the forest that now served as their sole path to survival. A darkly cloaked man who never spoke a word until Andree reached her destination met them. Shortly after she was safely transported out of Bouillon, some German soldiers came into the Florin's house and asked her father, "Where is your daughter?"

Auguste responded, "She has run away with her boyfriend." For some reason, they accepted that explanation and left. Auguste understood that his life could have ended right then and there. He prayed his rosary's black beads that night for forgiveness for lying and then prayed the white beads for his exiled daughter's safety.

Andree was safer while in France with Auguste's trusted associates. For several months, she was separated with no communication allowed back to her own family. It troubled her that she didn't even get an explanation of why she needed to go to France again, and this time by herself. The only thing that her father would tell her was that it was for her own safety. She fully trusted her father to protect her and she accepted his intuition. Auguste felt that her fragile heart had already been bruised with the news of the violence happening in their village and felt that if he also had to explain to her the soldier's exploits of rape and abuse, it would only add to her distress.

It was important that Andree didn't know too much about what was going on. With knowledge of his involvement with the resistance, it might be possible for the German soldiers to get secrets from her by threatening her life, so Auguste purposely kept her out of the loop. Mom says that children were often targeted with threats to try to get them to tell on their parents. Some of the children did tell about their parent's activities when German soldiers threatened them. While the children were rewarded with food or candy, their parents were typically arrested and sent away to labor camps.

Andree returned from France when the Germans stopped taking young girls. An English soldier had made the trek into France accompanied by a French soldier. They took her to the border at night where they met Auguste. There, Andree was reunited with her father in the darkness of the eerie forest. Unfortunately, after arriving home, Andree found her home life even more distorted. A bomb had destroyed her childhood home and the family had moved to the villa up on the hill overlooking the town. To see her childhood home lie in a pile of rubble turned her grief into anger at those who'd taken her lifelong security from her. Andree's feelings of rage would fester but never be allowed to show or even be talked about.

The Germans had issued a rule that the doors on every house would remain unlocked. If anyone violated the rules, they would be shot. One day, a soldier came to the house of Andree's cousin, a young nine-year-old boy. For some reason, he had locked the door. When a Nazi soldier came to it, he couldn't open it and yelled to the residents to open it. The young boy may have been just fooling around, but when he opened the door, the soldier scolded him for locking it. He then shot and killed him on the spot.

There was again no recourse. Belgian nationals just did what they were ordered to do or else they faced the consequences. Andree was becoming resentful over how the Germans treated the villagers. Instead of winning over the populace, the invaders created a deeper hatred for Hitler and his propaganda. News of this event made Andree even more resolute to keep her growing list of secrets from the soldiers.

There were sympathizers in Belgium who thought that Hitler's ideals were acceptable. One such sympathizer, who had early on gotten the attention of the Fuehrer, was Leon Degrelle. He had been communicating his neo-socialist ideas to Hitler and Mussolini over the preceding years. They both supported his Rexist movement and even gave him money. Mr. Degrelle had even been asked by Hitler to help form a huge army to invade Russia. In history books, this event is recorded still as the largest army to ever assemble and march into war (Degrelle). Mr. Degrelle, a Walloon, had changed from being a friend to a traitor in the eyes of Andree and her family. Mom says that the reason Hitler even had any interest in her village was because of Degrelle. While historical accounts don't tell that story, it well could have played a part in why Bouillon was so attractive to the Germans. The prevailing thought as to why Hitler sought control of the Ardennes was because of its location, which, once occupied, would help to drive a wedge between France and England.

On one particular evening, while I was sitting at my computer doing some reading up on the history of World War II, I found a story about Rexism and the million-man army that marched west to Russia. "Mom," I called, "have you ever heard of this man called Leon Degrelle?"

She became very incensed at me and you could almost feel the anger. "He was a traitor," she replied. "He was a family friend that we trusted, until he turned to Hitler. Most people in the town hated him because he brought Hitler to Bouillon. One Sunday he came to church with his uniform on knowing that all uniforms of the Nazis were banned in the church services. The priest threw him out of the service, and in response Leon Degrelle had the priest publicly beaten. The Catholic Church excommunicated him for this action. He is one of the three men I hate. They ruined my life."

This conversation totally took me by surprise. I had never heard Mom say that she hated anyone until now. Wow, she had just told me that there were three men that she hated. That meant that she still harbored resentment for what happened in her hometown during the war. I began to understand Mom better that night. I began to see that these men who "ruined her life" had not then, and never would, get her forgiveness. She is the only one who holds the power to offer up her forgiveness for their crimes. Albeit, all of these evil men have passed away, she still holds the one thing from them that they can't control or take away. She is still standing, and in a way, victorious in her own right because she withholds that forgiveness.

I then asked Mom if she could ever forgive Hitler for what he had done. I had no idea what a foolish and selfish question I was asking. No one in his or her right mind would ever ask her this question, but I was beginning to wonder if this was holding her heart captive in a place that didn't allow her to let go of the past. She was not willing at this time to even discuss or consider forgiveness. She dodged the question at first, but then said, "Maybe at some point in my life, I will be able to. I don't know."

By now, I was feeling the intensity grow and I knew it was time to let the subject go for both of our sakes. It was obviously painful for her. Now I was starting to feel remorseful for even trying to get her to answer that question. Who was I, and what have I ever experienced that ever qualified me to approach a war survivor with perhaps the most difficult question anyone could ever try to answer? I was the one needing to ask for her forgiveness now.

The picture of Mom's life became a little bit clearer to me on that day, and I realized that my whole understanding of her was being transformed. I was being changed.

I was experiencing what I once heard described as, "being so close to someone that you can taste the salt in their tears." I was touching the very delicate nerves that were protected by the thinnest of covering and I realized now that I had better tread carefully and through this maze of experiences.

4. DEFIANT EYES

L iving in occupied Belgium was certainly a bitter pill to swallow. Andree's beautiful homeland was being destroyed bit by bit. Bombs rained down on the town over and over. First the Germans bombed the village to soften up the resistance. It was during one of these early bombing raids that the Florin's home and businesses in the village were destroyed. Fortunately, because her parents had done well with those businesses, they also owned a villa that was not destroyed, on the hill overlooking the town.

The family lived in the villa over the next four years. They lived in the basement mostly to avoid being killed from bombs. The thought that the family might survive a bomb dropped directly on their house from an airplane that is thousands of feet in the sky is hard to understand. Regardless of the odds, all of the residents still took every possible opportunity to increase their chances of coming out of the war alive.

With the Germans now fully in control of Bouillon, the bombing started raining down again, but now it came from the Allied forces trying to dislodge the Nazis. This was the unfortunate consequence of living so close to the German border. The Nazis pushed over the border, and then the Allies tried to drive them back. Belgium was a focal point of strategic importance to both sides of the war because of its central location between France and England.

Under rules of the occupation, many things were different. Not only did the war take away Andree's childhood home, it was chipping away at her dreams, and she knew it. Day in and day out, another piece of her life was removed. Her freedoms, which she cherished most as a young and carefree flower-picking *Great Granddaughter of the Duke*, were escaping her grasp. No matter how hard she tried, she couldn't hold onto them. Regardless of the destruction and desperation everywhere, she indignantly maintained that they would never take away her pride. It may be the last thing she owned, but it was hers, and they would never get that. Eleanor Roosevelt was quoted to have said, "Nobody can make you feel inferior without your permission (Roosevelt)." This statement epitomizes the girl caught in the crossfire and the Mom I remember growing up with. Ralph Waldo Emerson wrote, "To be yourself in a world that is constantly trying to make you something else is the greatest accomplishment (Emerson)."

The new laws were very stringent. Curfews had to be obeyed. The doors could never be locked. The window shades and all the curtains were removed from all of the houses. This was so that the soldiers could keep an eye on everyone. There would be no smiling, no laughing, and no loud noises. No hammers could be used, and even the pots and pans were not to be banged together. That also meant that there would be no celebrating like laughing, playing games outside, or listening to music. Andree was not allowed to play the piano that she had studied for many years in school. She loved playing her piano, but the rules of survival meant she would have to give that up too. There would be no more Beethoven, no more Bach, and certainly, no more music of great inspiration by Mozart!

The soldiers stole everything and anything. They took the food, the batteries, the fuel, and basically helped themselves to whatever they wanted. Even though there was little to eat, if a soldier came into the home, there was no concern for the hungry children. The food would be given to him in exchange for not being beaten with the butt end of the rifle, whipped, or even shot. When I asked Mom how they survived she said, "We were lucky. We knew a farmer that would sneak an egg or two to the house. We made grass soup too."

It made me wonder, "If they were the lucky ones, what did the unlucky ones eat?"

Andree was learning how to tiptoe through this minefield of invaders. Inside, she hated every bit of the soldiers' presence, but outwardly, she gave them what they asked for without argument. In this new world order, cooperation was the key to survival.

Mom was taught to never look into the eyes of a passing soldier. It was forbidden. When she walked by a soldier, she looked down into the gutter in an act of submission. Even the sidewalks were made off limits to the town residents. The villagers were forced to walk in the streets or in the gutters, while the sidewalks were for the soldiers only. It was one more step to try and demoralize the residents and one more reason for her to resent the occupiers.

One day when Mom and her mother decided to go outside for some fresh air, Andree was feeling a little bit of pride and independence about being able to walk with her mother. She took the occasion to show her mom how she could express herself, and in a dangerous rebellious act, she maneuvered her feet up over the edge of the sidewalk and onto it. She had no trouble getting her feet over the edge of this threshold! Her mother yelled at her, "Get off of the sidewalk immediately," but Andree found this act of defiance very fulfilling.

As she was telling me about this, it reminded me of Rosa Parks, the African American woman who refused to give up her seat to a white passenger in the segregated city of Montgomery, Alabama (5). In the racially charged days of southern segregation, this could get you killed. It is that kind of righteous defiance that describes the mother I grew up with. I think I understand why she would do this and other defiant things growing up. Even during her stay in Maine, at eighty-four years of age, the remnants of an indomitable pride were present.

Just as Andree's mother was yelling for her to get off of the sidewalk, a German soldier turned the corner and saw her. Fear gripped them both because they knew what happened to their cousin for even a small violation of the rules. Andree quickly stepped off of the walkway and back into the gutter. With their eyes looking downward, they walked as though nothing was wrong, but then they heard a loud voice commanding them, "Kommen Sie Hier!"

Andree's mother understood the German language and could speak it quite fluently. The soldier was furious, and as they approached, he took his rifle from his shoulder, slipped a single bullet into the chamber, and pointed it at Andree's head.

"I will shoot your daughter now," he screamed.

Grandmother pleaded with him in his own language to please let her live. She knelt down at his feet and pleaded for mercy, in hopes that she might save her foolish little girl.

"She was only playing," Elizabeth cried. "Please, don't shoot my little child."

After waiting for a while with both of them crying and pleading for her life, the young soldier must have felt satisfied to have just instilled the fear of the Gestapo in them. He again warned them, "Stay in the gutters."

He told them that their next violation would bring an instant punishment. Then he walked away leaving both of them in tears and in shock. The emotions were almost more than her mother could bear. The experience tore even deeper into Andree's heart, leaving yet another imprint that would become a tattered thread in the fabric of her life.

During the altercation Grandmother worried that Andree would be forced to look into the soldier's eyes. She knew that the pent up anger fomenting in Andree's heart could be seen in her eyes, and she worried that if the Germans saw this, they might push her to a breaking point where she would reveal more about her father's work with the resistance. Could she hold it together and keep hidden her knowledge that her father was in some way connected to the Maquis?

I've heard it said that the eyes are the windows of the soul. In this case, it was imperative that no one look too closely into Andree's eyes. As much as possible, her mother kept her daughter inside and out of the presence of the enemy troops. Everyone was on edge, and it seemed every soldier was on a hair trigger. They were just itching to shoot someone to prove their dominance. Elizabeth knew how close she came to losing her daughter that day and she didn't want to repeat that situation ever again.

I discovered another memento in Mom's boxes. The paragraph she penned stated that she was afraid for her life. It says that her mother told her and her siblings to, "Be careful of the German soldiers. Don't get mad, don't talk to them, and don't do anything foolish!" It appears that Mom was becoming overwhelmed with the treatment given them by the occupying soldiers and it became harder and harder for her to follow her mother's advice.

With so much going wrong in her life, Andree wondered where the hero was that she had placed all of her youthful hopes in. She reflected on her circle of friends from school and from town and was curious how they were surviving this horrible war. She had not seen many of them for a long time. She knew that the Germans had burned down two of her best friends' homes because their parents were suspected of helping the resistance. Mom ached for a return to the home life she loved not long before.

To escape for a while from the despair, Andree would go back in her mind to the days of castles and knights. She remembered how she had put pictures of some of her friends into her white pocketbook. She prayed for them, even though rumors had spread that some of them were no longer alive. "Don't worry," she said. "We will all be together again after this is over, and I will spend time with you doing all the things we loved to do before this war began."

Day after long day, Mom used these dreams and prayers to transcend from her grim surroundings to a place of serenity filled with fields of hope and happier times. Unfortunately, it would be a long while before those times returned.

5. UNEXPECTED GUEST

Every night, Andree knelt down with the rest of her family to recite the prayers she'd learned as a young girl in Catholic school. As she passed each rosary bead through her fingers she dedicated that prayer to a face she had not seen in a while. She moved her fingers to the next black bead on her rosary and continued until every bead was finished. There were so many faces that flashed in her mind. More often than not, it seemed there were not enough rosary beads to cover the missing acquaintances.

One very cold day in December, Andree discovered first hand why so many people were missing. She and her family were trying to stay warm inside the basement of their villa when they heard trucks and a commotion in the street just outside the home. As she peaked out the window, she saw a large German truck picking up men from Bouillon. She noticed that some of the men were Jewish. They were identifiable by the yellow star they had to sew onto their sleeves. One of the men was the local businessman who had become good friends with the family. "Why would they take him?" She wondered. He was not part of the secret resistance, she thought. He was a nice man with a very nice family. Come to think of it, she had not seen his family either for a long time.

Mom wanted to scream at seeing this unjust removal of men from her town. Of course, she could be punished for making noise, so she only screamed on the inside. The men, guarded by German soldiers with rifles, were being herded like animals into the truck. Mom reflected that all of the ladies and their children were crying and one woman was handing her husband a blanket. With temperatures being so cold, Mom felt that this was little consolation. She wondered about the conditions where they were being taken. Her father tried to assure her that they would return after working in a remote part of Germany. The men were told that they would be helping to fight the enemy by working hard for the Fuehrer at a labor camp.

I've seen pictures of the labor camps. The signs outside read *Arbeit Macht Frei*, translated, *Work Makes You Free*. Of course, if you read about what really happened at the labor camps, you'll discover that millions of men, women and children perished from disease, starvation, cold, firing squads, and gas chambers (7). In one of history's darkest hours, there lived an evil beyond words. The world saw an army so trained to hate, kill, and destroy that other people's lives became meaningless to them. Innocent villagers whose lives had once been an important part of society were ripped from their peaceful existence, thrown into these prison camps, and treated worse than dogs. It is beyond the grasp of comprehension.

Mom had seen enough at this point to perhaps never recover sufficiently to live a carefree life. Her bombed out home with her cherished memories was gone forever. She'd lost her friends and relatives and wondered if it could get any worse. Must her mind be scarred by any more violence and hatred? As she prayed for the violence to end, Mom still held out hope for her country. After all, she was a *Great Granddaughter of the Duke*. There was no quitting in her. Mom saw this special trait in Godfroi, then in her father, and she wanted to be just like them. Her father was a brave man by the mere fact that he was helping the resistance. When he had to lie to the Germans to save his daughter, he showed her that some things are more important than the truth. His life was a lie on a day-to-day basis, and she learned to accept that it was necessary for survival.

The war seemed to linger on and on with little to feel positive about. If not for the secret radio in the basement, there would be nothing but gloom. Fortunately, once in a while, Auguste could tell some news to the family about things he'd heard of some military successes the Americans were having. Basically, life settled into a lull for weeks on end, broken up only by Sunday Mass. Andree would sit at home and read a lot. Sometimes it felt safe to let Andree stay home alone while the rest of the family went out. It was during one of these times that there was an unexpected guest.

A stern knock at the door caused Andree to quickly bounce up from her reading and open the unlocked door. Standing at the entrance to the house was the most fearful image she could have ever imagined. A uniformed Nazi soldier's frame filled the doorway. Instant shock ran through her veins. Seeing the uniform itself was sufficient to draw a wide array of emotions. Hate, fear, anger, and even nausea, were just a few of the feelings Mom said the uniform evoked from her. The Swastika insignia showing on the sleeves of the soldier almost made her heart stop

The Swastika, the symbol of the Nazi regime, with its backwards-crossed pattern actually had its origins in the Iron Age. It was a sign of health, prosperity, and hope, and that symbol was being used to further Fascist Nazi ambitions.

The German soldier moved into her dining room, waving his arms and speaking to her in a language that she didn't understand. He was obviously very upset. It didn't matter that there was a serious communication breakdown between them because what she did understand was that he was holding a hand grenade and he was threatening to blow up the house. Andree worried for her life and began to silently ask God to protect her. So many thoughts rushed through her mind that she could barely think, not the least was that it was finally her turn to join the growing list of Bouillon's dead and missing.

The soldier was now pointing to the upstairs bedroom and Andree acted confused but feared the worst of his intentions knowing how these soldiers treated other young girls. After some frantic expressions and hand gestures, along with some disconnected attempts at conversation, it appeared as though the young soldier was just asking for a place to sleep. He motioned for Andree to remain downstairs and indicated that he would sleep upstairs. He warned that if the family attempted anything foolish, he would pull the pin from the grenade.

When Andree's family arrived home, she explained to them that there was a German soldier upstairs sleeping with a live grenade in his hand and that he would blow them up if he felt threatened. Auguste must have turned white at the thought of the soldier looking around in the basement. Worse than that was his remorse for leaving his daughter alone at home to confront the soldier. Knowing how much she had been through, it must have been like an arrow being shot through his heart to realize he had let down his guard. Auguste had let his daughter take the brunt of this confrontation alone, and it pained him greatly. He hugged Andree with all his might in an effort to show her how much he loved her. He begged her forgiveness and she readily gave it to him. Then they walked down the stairs to the basement together.

That night the family slept on pins and needles, if at all. They often slept with their clothes on, not knowing if and when they would need to get out quickly. The secret radio was moved to a place that would make it unlikely to be found, and they waited for the soldier to leave.

When morning came, the soldier was heard walking down the stairs, leaving through the front door, and slamming it behind him. He didn't say anything in parting, which was fine with Auguste. After it was silent for a while, Auguste searched the bedroom he had slept in to make sure it was safe. Nothing but an unmade bed was left behind. Mom said that the soldier looked as though he was scared and she thought that perhaps he wanted to escape the German army. Sadly, many young boys were recruited into Hitler's forces. Whatever his motivation was, it was a very scary experience for the Florin family.

I have some personal experience with a live hand grenade. I can tell you that having someone who is losing touch with reality, holding a grenade in a threatening manner would be an extremely frightening experience.

I enlisted in the US Army right out of high school. When I graduated from Norwich Regional Technical School in 1973, I was already a Private Second Class. This was due to an early enlistment option. I was sent to train at Fort Dix, New Jersey, and wanted to qualify on every type of weapon I could. I received a certificate for being a sharpshooter with the M-16 rifle, and I received training with the M-60 machine gun. All was going well until I held a couple of live hand grenades in my hands.

In order to qualify for grenade throwing, a recruit had to have one grenade in their belt clip and one in their hand. While the trainee stood there with the sergeant by his side, he was required to pull the pin and hold it back by his head while he counted to three, slowly. Then he is required to throw it about seventy-five feet away at a predetermined target and immediately duck down into the cement shelter that had a two inch thick Plexiglas window to watch through. If any mistakes were made, it could cost one's life.

The drill sergeant told us that only a few boys had died from making mistakes over the previous ten years, so our odds of success were very high. I guess I had watched just one too many war movies because I always thought that once the pin was pulled, the grenade had only seconds to explode. The truth is that you can hold the lever down for as long as you want. The grenade will only blow up three seconds after the lever is released.

After pulling the pin from the grenade, I freaked out! There was no way I was going to hold a live grenade next to my head and calmly count, one, two, three, then throw it at a distant target. I tossed the grenade about fifteen feet from where my drill sergeant and I were standing. Seeing how I had done this, he immediately pushed me down into the shelter and we both covered our ears. Ka-boom! Shrapnel splattered the wall in front of us. The explosion sounded like thunder being so close. I thought it was pretty cool, but the drill sergeant reached over and grabbed my other grenade. He told me to stay in the pit. He then pulled the pin and launched it downfield. After it exploded and the area was safe, he said, "Bannon, you just failed to qualify in grenade tossing."

I was okay with that. I joined the army to be a communications expert, not a bomb thrower, anyhow.

For Mom, hearing these types of explosions was pretty common. Over the years, she became accustomed to the multitude of sounds. She could discern the distinct sounds of bombers overhead and knew when to take cover. She also knew the sounds of a German firing his rifle. This typically meant someone was just executed. She knew the sounds of warfare and could tell which engine drones were from a panzer tank or a loading truck. The routine air raid sirens warned when it was time to hide and when it was safe to come out of hiding. The ritual was very well rehearsed over the slowly passing days, weeks, months, and years in occupied Belgium.

It seemed her broken heart could not break anymore, nor could the bleak situation be more desperate. Mom got used to losing friends. Sometimes the Germans would come into the church with their guns in hand in the middle of a service looking for men or women that they wanted to take away. The ones they took from church were never seen again. They usually left the younger ones alone. Mom had become well rehearsed at looking young. Having a small build made it easier for her mother to disguise her into looking too young for the German's interest.

Another means the Germans used for collecting men, women, and children for sending to the labor camps, was to drive around the village with loud speakers and announce names of people who were to report to the church. Once there, they were either killed for being suspected of helping the Maquis or herded into trucks to be deported. Since the Germans had killed all of the police in the town, there was no recourse for these atrocities. There was no balance, nor was there fairness or reason. Fairness only lived in her dreams, while forgiveness remained sequestered in her heart.

During more contemporary conflicts in Iraq and Afghanistan, the world would see a military tribunal if troops were found to be doing things like insulting prisoners or embarrassing them. In Andree's war, these types of war crimes were mere child's play. Andree's war involved things like burning churches down filled with villagers. Its level of abuse went far beyond anything a progressive society could imagine. World War II has been represented in history as the most violent and horrific war ever. It saw some sixty million deaths that were related to the war in one way or another. The small neutral country of Belgium alone lost an estimated eighty-eight thousand lives. Sadly, seventy-seven thousand of those lost were civilians, and many were her acquaintances. (Wikipedia).

6. DEGRELLE'S REVENGE

In what was becoming a bitter battle of wills between the Belgian Resistance and Hitler's favorite Walloon, Leon Degrelle became one of the most hated men in Bouillon. Having grown up as friends with the Florin family, Leon and his brother, Edward, followed different paths in life. Edward continued the pharmacy business that his father had started. He served the town of Bouillon well and was loved by all the residents. On the other hand, Leon had become a political leader. He wrote books and gave speeches to promote his Rexist Party. His leanings gained him favor by Fascist leaders like Mussolini and Hitler. His goal was to eventually create a separate country for Walloons. Before his ambitions could be fulfilled, Leon would work his way through the ranks of the German Waffen SS all the way to becoming a general in Hitler's Army. He became so well liked by Hitler that at a ceremony where Leon was receiving a promotion, Hitler was quoted to have said, "If I had a son, I would have liked him to be like you (Degrelle)."

Leon's Rexists were not liked by the Maquis. They felt that he had sold out to the Nazis. Having been born in Bouillon and being a Walloon, he caused intense resentment among those fighting to survive the occupation.

In one of the boxes of memories Mom had so carefully collected and carted with her through many moves, I found a dozen torn and fragmented pages of notes that she had written at several different periods over the last thirty to forty years. None of the pages were dated, yet they all told the same story. Some were detailed and others were only touching the key points of the events. They all overlapped each other with slight variations. The following story represents these collective notes and mementoes in her words.

I heard gunfire coming from the town. I looked out my balcony and from there I saw a big commotion. It wasn't long before word spread that Edward Degrelle had been killed.

"Why?" I cried.

He was a good man, with a nice wife and family. There was no reason for this act of violence. Soon the news of his death travelled and many friends stopped by the drug store to see for themselves. Even my sister, Elizabeth, at only fourteen years old, went in to see what happened. She ran out of the store crying and went to get Father and tell him the terrible news.

By now I wanted to get to town to see for myself, but my father met Elizabeth and I at the bridge and told us to return home in a voice that suggested the outcome of this crime would be bad for everyone. The news struck me, "Like a tight hand on my throat."

With word of the murder spreading around, there were thoughts that Leon Degrelle would exact revenge for the killing of his brother. People ran around trying to hide. It was common knowledge that Leon was in Brussels, which was only a couple hours away. Soon, there would be a visit from our number one enemy, and the town folks were bracing for it.

Heading back home, we passed Edward Degrelle's wife, who was running to the store. Her face was filled with tears. My heart ached for her. Over and over I asked Father who would ever do this to such a good man. Father had no answers.

In almost two hours to the minute, two motorcycles arrived in the town to report Leon Degrelle's first order. All men between the ages of eighteen and thirty-five were to report to the Hotel De Panorama. They were also warned that if they did not go to the hotel, they would take the women and children.

I watched as one by one, men walked by with their wives and children up the pitiful road to their destination. There was a sobering sadness in their eyes, and their heads hung low as in resignation to their fate. Most of them held blankets in their hands.

One man tried to plead with the soldiers, explaining that his wife was soon going to have a baby, but it was useless. Once they realized the soldiers wouldn't help them, his very pregnant wife ran all the way back to their home to get his blanket. Upon returning, she tightened her lips to keep from showing her emotions. Crying would only make it harder for the husbands. These women were so courageous not to grieve in front of the Germans. They knew it would only give more satisfaction to them. This was very painful for me to watch.

One young eighteen year old boy ran away by climbing over a roof. Suddenly, bullets flew in his direction, but he escaped. The brave youth lived through it and I hope to someday meet him. He was very courageous, just like Duke Godfrod De Bouillon.

The rest of the men were loaded into trucks and taken away. I didn't know where they were taken but I assumed they were taken to labor camps.

The next order soon came from Degrelle, who had now arrived in Bouillon. The soldiers were to take away all of the bicycles, radios, typewriters, and even cars. No one would be allowed to leave the town. This infuriated me so much that I decided to bring my brother's baby bicycle to them. Mother warned me not to let my feelings cause me to do something stupid but I had seen enough, and it was time to retaliate by venting my anger. I waited until my mother's guard was down. When she wasn't watching I snuck out of the house, grabbed my little brother Pierre's bicycle and walked towards the soldier at the street corner.

As I approached the tall slender soldier, I began to get nervous. I eventually got close enough to see his blue eyes. He had a scar on his right cheek and also had a small whip at his side. I mustered all of my patriotic courage and threw the bike down in front of him. I said, "I suppose you need this, too!"

I didn't finish the statement by spitting at him because of the fire now in his eyes. He motioned with his hand that he was going to use his whip, so I turned and walked away. I heard him yell at me, "Get out!" I was lucky to not have been whipped.

Leon's next act of revenge was to have the other pharmacist in town killed. Mom's notes detail the emotions of this vengeful act with a pain wrought from war.

The soldiers woke up the pharmacist in the middle of the night and told him he was needed in town. He got up and started to leave, but his wife pleaded with him to stay home. She had a bad premonition about this. The faithful pharmacist told her that he was needed in town and that he must go. He was always willing to help others in need. When he opened the door to leave, he was met by two German soldiers who shot him several times. He was badly wounded, but he didn't die immediately.

I recall that he suffered a long time that night. I heard the mournful crying of his wife echo for seemingly endless hours. The poor woman kept pleading for someone, anyone, to help him, but everyone was afraid to respond with the Germans standing guard everywhere. The pharmacist eventually died in her arms. I felt her pain, but I couldn't help.

Sunday arrived the next day and the residents were allowed to attend church. It was the only time we were able to find a little peace and strength. During the service however, we heard the distinct sounds of Army boots walking on the old wooden church floor. There was no trouble discerning that sound. The soldiers had come into the church and were taking people out again. They were getting closer to me, when suddenly I realized that I had forgotten my identification card. They always checked ID's. My heart stopped for a second knowing what they would do to me without an ID. I slumped into my pew bench in an attempt to look smaller than I was. I was small to begin with, and Mother tried to dress me to look even younger, to avoid being questioned as an adult. At almost eighteen years old, I looked only thirteen. The soldiers walked by after glancing at me and then left the church. "Another miracle," I thought.

After church, our family was walking over the bridge to go home and noticed that there were three men lined up by soldiers against the wall. I just couldn't look at them. I was already feeling ill over the incident in the church, so I kept walking without turning back. I didn't know what was happening to those men.

Later in the week, my father decided to take the family to the Semois River for a swim so that we might get a break from all of the depressing events happening in Bouillon. On the way home, I saw some of my girlfriends walking in town. When we met, my three friends told me that they had lost their fathers to the Nazis. These fathers were three important men in Bouillon. They were executed for helping the Maquis. It turns out that they were taken into the woods and shot like animals. Then they were thrown onto a wagon and returned to their families. There was a small thin red trail of blood that followed the wagon's path from the woods all the way back to their homes.

After this vengeful killing, a funeral was held for the three men. All of the town's women paid their respects to their fallen leaders' families. I watched the procession from my balcony.

No one stopped to visit Leon Degrelle even though his brother had died also. This caused him to become more incensed. He gave a new order that all of the town's residents were required to come and pay their respects to his family. The villagers would have gone to his home before, had they not been so afraid of Leon. That evening, some ladies went to his home and even sang a song to the Degrelle family. Leon saw in their eyes, however, that they were not as sincere as he wished. He wanted them to grieve as they had grieved for those three men.

This lack of concern from the church and villagers caused Leon Degrelle to have the priest arrested and brought to his home, where he would remain under house arrest indefinitely. Perhaps Degrelle felt that the priest didn't do enough to encourage the residents to mourn his brother's life like they mourned the others. The killing of his brother seemed to drive Leon nearly insane with bitterness.

Eventually, Leon Degrelle had to return to Brussels where his Rexists followers were strongest. When he finally left, the priest was released to go back to serving the remaining members of his parish.

This tit-for-tat episode of violence certainly left its impression on the hearts of all of Bouillon's residents. Degrelle got his blood vengeance satisfied but left his hometown a hated man, never to return again. He escaped the Allies after the war when he crash-landed his plane in San Sebastian, Spain, where the Spanish government offered him asylum. There he continued to espouse his Rexist ideals and write about his philosophies. There was an attempt to kidnap him to bring him to justice in Belgium, but that attempt failed. Later in life he was interviewed by a newspaper journalist in Spain and he was asked about his regrets. His response was, "Only that we lost (germandagger.com)." Leon died in 1994 at the age of eighty-seven years old.

This chapter's events are the only ones that were recorded using Mom's written notes and strung in succession as well as possible. I called Mom to confirm the accuracy of these events but she could not remember them. She did admit that she did many things when she was young similar to what I had written about her in this chapter. Had I not found these notes, I would not have known how well she knew one of Hitler's main protégés. These events could have been lost forever save for a plain white envelope stuffed with the folded and tattered memos about Leon's revenge.

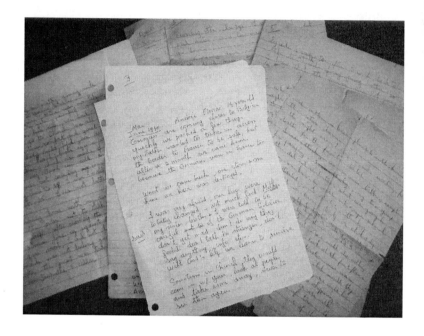

7. HITLER'S ANGER

One Spring day in 1945 would be a day when time stood still. For Mom it was a day that she wished could be as distant to her memories as the amount of years that have passed since then. Auguste had been next door in the basement with his neighbor, who had his own secret radio tuned in to an English broadcast. They were listening to the messages coming over the static filled transmissions and had just found out that the Americans had landed at Normandy. Auguste was so excited that he almost forgot the Germans were still in control of Bouillon. He ran out of his neighbor's house and ran over to his house to tell his family the good news. They were all very excited but reminded their father, "Remain calm, don't look happy, and don't do anything foolish."

Secretly, word spread to others in town that the Americans were coming, but it was important for everyone to pretend that everything was still the same. A little gloating in front of a soldier was a dangerous thing, maybe even more so now that the Germans were facing an inevitable attack from the advancing Allies.

It would take time, but there was reason for hope. The Americans would finally be pushing towards Bouillon. After almost four years, there was a glimmer of light breaking through this recurring nightmare.

The resistance effort had taken its toll on the weary Germans. They had lost many men during the war on both borders of Germany. The Russians had taken back most of their country and were pushing towards Berlin. The Allies were pushing towards Berlin from France's coast. Hitler decided to send most of his remaining forces up the Ardennes in one final effort to head off the American's advance. Bouillon sat right in the middle of the conflict.

In what was to become one of World War II's worst battles as far as lives lost, the Battle of the Bulge was formed. It created a huge bulge in the Allied lines as Nazi forces swelled their ranks from the Ardennes to the center of Belgium, hoping to separate the whole of France from the Allies at the coast. Nineteen thousand soldiers died in this fight alone. It was one of the coldest and snowiest battles that Hitler and the Americans had ever fought. To say that the snow was a Godsend for the Allies would be inaccurate, because this bitter winter hit the American forces equally hard.

While the major concern for Hitler was his retreating battle lines, the occupying soldiers decided they would take one final act of revenge on Bouillon due to the fact that they knew there were still resistance fighters hiding there. Degrelle hated the thought that after four years of trying to subjugate the Belgians, they did not just roll over and accept their defeat. The feelings of hatred were mutual.

In what Andree calls the worst night of the war, their final act was also her most vivid.

On that momentous day the German soldiers went to all of the households looking for gasoline. The soldiers collected gas from everywhere. At first it seemed that they intended to fuel their trucks for a long mission, but the way they placed the cans all around the village spoke otherwise. Auguste soon discovered that due to the hatred the soldiers had for the people of Bouillon and the villager's unwillingness to submit entirely to the will of the Fuehrer, the town was to be burned to the ground. Everyone in the town would pay the ultimate price. The orders also warned that anyone trying to escape would be shot. The question passed through Andree's mind, "Which was the better death, a bullet in the head, or slowly burning to death?"

This type of atrocity had been carried out in other places during the war and the stories are well documented. In Oradour Sur Glane, France, not far from Bouillon, there was a massacre in a church. It was filled with people, and then grenades were tossed into the windows. As men, women, and children tried to escape the inferno, they were shot (scrapbookpages.com). Mom wondered if this would be how she and her family would finally end their lives together.

The soldiers went about their heartless work placing the gas cans strategically around the town to ensure the most effective carnage. Peeking out of the window, Mom could see the location of a couple of the cans. Unfortunately, there was nothing she could do with Nazi soldiers on guard at every corner.

Accepting their ultimate demise, that night Andree and her family huddled into their basement. They shared their love for each other with words of forgiveness. Auguste had done all he could do to protect his family. He had managed to keep them safe during the entire occupation, and now there was no more protection that he could offer them. His arms encircled his children the best he could so as to show in his heart how much he cared for them. There were tears and inexplicable heartache as each family member tried to speak but became choked by the welling up anguish. The only consolation for them at this point was that they had fought the fight as a family and would die together as a family.

Outside, trucks rumbled through the night making so much noise that it seemed the walls of the villa would crumble. Each minute seemed like an eternity as they snuggled together for one last evening. As the minutes dragged into hours, they waited for the fires to begin. Finally, the tired eyes of the children couldn't stay open any longer. Auguste and Elizabeth were able to remain awake and still pass the rosary beads between their fingers. Mom recalled that her mother and father prayed for one more miracle. Auguste had given all he had for his country. Just like Godfroi, he fought to his last bit of strength. The war had taken its toll on Auguste. He was growing weak and frail, but he still proved with his remaining strength that he would give everything he had left to make his family feel loved on their final night.

At some point during the darkness, the town became eerily quiet. The Germans finished moving all of their trucks out of the town to avoid being caught in the inferno. Auguste kept his eyes fixed to the clock on the shelf that showed it was early morning. It was dark outside and all of the children were still sleeping. Then like a rolling plague, Auguste heard the sound of screams coming from the village below. He snuggled with his wife and kids as close as is physically possible, looking into the tear-filled eyes of Elizabeth with final release. He had no regrets, nor did she. He loved his family to the end and was so proud of them. They were at peace with their fate now.

The screams from the village grew closer and louder and the pitched darkness began to glow. Auguste heard the familiar rumble of tanks outside which shook the house and woke up the children. Surprised that they were still alive, the children begged their father to go upstairs and look out the windows. After Auguste's sleepless night, dawn was approaching. Reluctantly at first, fearing what they might see, then finally relenting to their pleas, Auguste, Elizabeth, and the children went upstairs to sneak a look. When they looked out into the dimly lit dawn, they collectively gasped at the sight. "Oh my God, what is going on?" they all wondered.

The huge imposing figure of an army tank sat right in front of their house!

I have personally experienced the fear that a German army tank can instill in a person. When I was on one of our field exercises during my two-year tour of duty in Germany, I decided to take a little unauthorized stroll through the woods. When I looked into a small clearing, I saw a German tank with its long gun barrel pointed at me. "Uh, oh," I thought.

As I walked up the hill, the barrel kept its sights on me. Even though we were all supposed to be allies as we did this joint forces training exercise together, I still feared that the soldier in the tank might want to experiment with firing off a blank round just to see my reaction. I think I would probably have died from a heart attack if he had done that.

Andree now feared that another atrocity was about to take place when the gun barrel rotated towards their home where little faces filled the window panes. As quickly as the turret turned, the cover slowly lifted open and the soldier looked down at the whole family all scrunched together in the little window. For a moment the Florin family was confused. Then, like a morning sun warms the cool dawn, the soldier offered up a big smile and then waved to them. This was not a German soldier for sure they soon realized. Those soldiers didn't smile unless they were torturing someone. Behind the big smile Andree immediately noticed an American flag hanging inside the turret cover. Suddenly, an indescribable rush of emotion filled their hearts and an uncontrollable river of joy began to pour out of their eyes.

The screaming that they had heard approaching was the sounds of the entire village ablaze with the growing celebrations instead of ablaze with fires. The gasoline cans all still sat right where they had been placed, yet not one of them was ever lit. It seemed that the Germans were in such a hurry to get out of town, with the Allies advancing, that they left everything and ran.

It was the miracle Auguste had prayed for, and these American soldiers were the heroes that Andree had always dreamed would come to rescue her. She danced in the street and then jumped up and down on her sidewalk with reckless abandon. Andree and all of the town's residents hugged the American soldiers and cried with joy. The soldiers had chocolate and food rations that they shared with everyone. Food was in such demand that, immediately after the town was freed, the Allied forces dropped supplies and food from airplanes.

In the village, old men danced with children as they screamed at the top of their lungs, "The Americans have come! The Americans have come!" The nightmare was really over! There were celebrations everywhere as neighbors met throughout the day in the village. What began as the darkest night in the four-year occupation of Bouillon ended in the happiest day ever.

Shortly after the liberation, the Belgian government and the American soldiers decided to have a huge celebration in Bouillon. There was a dance held in the big ballroom of one of the hotels that had survived the war without damage. It was hosted to honor the Americans who rescued them from the edge of destruction. Auguste and Elizabeth were chaperones that evening. Mom recalled that it was so exciting to dance with the American soldiers. They were not very good at speaking French, but it was fun to listen to them try.

One soldier decided to try out his French on Andree. He said, "Voules vous chouches avec moi?" Mom was shocked by his statement that translates, "Would you like to go to bed with me?"

It was probably the only French that this young soldier knew. She was so upset that she walked away and left him standing there alone on the dance floor. After all, she was a naive girl raised by nuns and carefully guarded by her father.

Bouillon entered a time of rebuilding and healing, all of which held more surprises and sorrows than Andree could have imagined. On one sad day their Jewish friend, who'd been picked up by the German trucks on that cold night in December, came walking into the town alone. He looked broken and weak, hardly the man who was taken away from Bouillon during the height of its occupation. His eyes were darker and sunken and his cheeks appeared skeletal as though he had been starved nearly to death. Andree wondered what his eyes had seen. He asked if anyone knew where his family was. Andree and everyone else told him that they had not seen any of them since they disappeared. Auguste offered to help him find his wife and children, but the poor old man refused the help and just kept walking. He was never seen again. Mom wasn't sure if he walked until he found them, or if he walked until he died of exhaustion. He was so distraught that it was more likely that he might have died of a broken heart. He had nothing left to live for.

Seeing her family friend in such distress hurt Andree in ways she had not experienced before. The war was over, and people were celebrating. But while some were lucky to be alive, he was one of those that were still suffering. The healing was not going to happen for many who wondered whether their children were victims of a labor camp atrocity or if their families might still be alive. Andree wept for her friend openly. She wondered how fate could appoint to one person such pain, while she enjoyed such relief. It was a question she would not get answered in this life.

Another conflict arose with the town after the war. It was discovered that ten local girls had slept with German soldiers for money and food. There was a large commotion one night and Auguste heard about it. Some of the men were so upset with the girls that they had put swastikas on their foreheads and were going to kill them. When Auguste arrived, he spoke to the men and was able to change their minds. He defended the girls as being under immense pressure and told them to blame the Germans not the girls. Since he was a well-respected community member, all of the girl's lives were saved.

Auguste knew that to survive the occupation, people had to compromise their values. He never believed in lying, but to save his children's lives, he lied. He reasoned that with so much taken from everyone, it was time to focus on forgiveness and rebuilding. This meant turning their hearts and eyes and minds back to working as a community. It meant working together as they had before the Nazis took control their lives. The big question however was, could the citizens of Bouillon cast aside their hurts and judgments in order to focus on the work ahead?

8. LIFE WITH THE ALLIES

Rebuilding Bouillon would be a huge task, but the residents were ready for it. The houses that were destroyed would require extensive work and money. Since money was scarce, Auguste had not repaired the bombed out home in the village. The villa on the hill, where they lived for the last four years, was in good condition and would become the home Mom would spend the rest of her days in until she left Bouillon for good.

Life with the Americans seemed better day by day. Shoes, food, and other supplies came shortly after their arrival. Andree began to play her piano again and music filled the air as Bouillon changed from being an occupied town to being a liberated community. Although the wave of inhumanity had touched everyone, the new flood of appreciation for the Americans became stronger than all of the other emotions. Many of the American troops shared their free time with the villagers and many got to know the local families. These soldiers were warmly accepted, easily winning over the hearts of the Belgians.

In a way, I can relate to the townspeople wanting to get to know the Americans. They were the heroes. They came bearing gifts and smiles and best of all, freedom. Against the backdrop of Bouillon's war experiences, every American was a hero.

When I was an American soldier serving in Germany in 1976, well after the war, I remember how the locals appreciated our presence. During one particular German, French, and American field exercise, there were thousands of troops deployed across Germany practicing in a joint forces battlefield excursion called *Reforger*. It was on the same exercise that I had experienced the German tank hiding in the woods. This war rehearsal was in such a remote part of the country, that there were very few German nationals around. On this day however, my best friend and I saw an elderly lady working in the field with her daughters. Although it was not permissible to leave our encampment, he and I walked over to them and practiced speaking our broken German that we learned in army school.

"Guten tag," we said.

"Guten tag," we heard back.

Encouraged by this, we shared a few more words and laughs with them. They seemed very happy to have met us and invited us to dinner at their home that night. We agreed to try and be there. Besides, we didn't know how to say, in German, "It's against the rules."

I don't think we really wanted to refuse their invitation considering our alternative was to eat dinner from a tin can, looking at one hundred other camouflage dressed men, seated at ten makeshift picnic tables inside a smoke filled camouflage tent.

Under the cover of darkness that evening, my friend and I slipped out of the encampment and spent hours with the wonderful family in their home talking in broken English and broken Deutch. It was really fun and almost made me forget about the horribly muddy conditions in our field camp. As we were leaving we were invited to return the next evening. "It is against the rules," we tried to explain, but the opportunity to enjoy a few German beers and learn their language better was simply too hard to refuse.

Consequently, the next night, with two buddies now in tow, we left the camp and attended dinner with our new friends. These meetings continued for several more nights, and each time we would get questioned about whether we had ever entertained thoughts about marrying a German girl. I recall they had several daughters, but they were only in their younger teens. Maybe they thought that after we finished our enlistment, we might return and marry them? They were a really fun family for us to visit. We stayed in touch by mail for several years following our time in the army.

Back in Bouillon, on one beautiful afternoon, Mom was playing her piano when suddenly there was a knock at the door. When the door was opened, a soldier in full uniform with a rifle slung over his shoulder was standing there. At first, Mom's heart skipped a beat as she thought back to the image of the last time a uniformed soldier stood in her doorway. This time, though, was very different. The warmth of this soldiers' smile immediately spoke of friendship, so Auguste invited him in. The soldier explained that he had heard the piano playing from outside the home and that he would like permission to play it. He'd been consumed with his job of getting the Nazis out of Belgium and had not played a piano for a long time. Now, as a result of his good French speaking ability and Elizabeth's proficient English, they all enjoyed a special moment together.

It frustrated Mom, however, to listen to this man who could not even read music, play the piano so well. He played by ear. He played ragtime and boogie-woogie music and songs that they had never heard before. Andree, being a well-heeled student, was taught to read Mozart by the strictest of nuns. She thought that this was so wrong for the soldier to be able to play without the sheets of music to follow. However, he was a charming American hero, so she applauded his every performance. I think during that evening, she might also have dropped a few hints in his direction that she was still waiting for her hero to show up. She says that she didn't speak to him, but she certainly knew how to speak with her eyes.

When the soldier left the house, his parting words were, "I will return in three years and marry your daughter." He then looked over at Andree, smiled, and walked out.

Auguste, who now grinned from ear to ear, thought this was a superb opportunity, but Elizabeth was not so enthusiastic about it. Andree had never even said one word to the soldier, nor had he said anything to her, but his parting pronouncement left them all in awe. Andree wondered if it had really happened or if she had just dreamed it. She was really good at dreaming. In fact, she started to think of her childhood dreams again after this event. She tried to remember the notes that she had written and placed into her white pocketbook before the war. Unfortunately, those youthful ideals had long ago been crushed beneath the weight of the war machine. "Could this fairy tale love connection really be happening to me?" she wondered. She knew for sure, however, that this soldier's picture was not in her collection of faces she had saved.

A short time later, a letter arrived in the mail post marked from Germany. It was from the piano playing American soldier and it was addressed to Auguste and Elizabeth Florin. In the letter was a formal request for permission to marry their daughter. Auguste turned to Andree and asked her if she remembered the American. Mom had to laugh! "An American hero with a funny name, comes into our house, plays beautifully on the piano, and then announces plans to marry me. How could I forget that?" she replied.

Auguste asked her again, "Well, what do you think?"

With her head spinning, all she could do was fall back on her life-long ideals of one day marrying her hero.

"Yes, I will marry him!" she replied proudly.

The room filled with cheers and smiles, and Auguste wasted no time spreading the news that his daughter, Andree, would marry an American soldier. He was the proudest father in Bouillon that day!

Mom was now almost twenty years old and the next three years would be a challenge. She corresponded with her fiancé, but with his army base in Germany and her home in Belgium, it was a long and difficult engagement. She began to doubt whether she would ever marry him and even began to talk to another nice young man from Bouillon. This man also wished to have her hand in marriage, but Auguste reminded Andree about her commitment.

Almost three years after the end of the war the quiet in the home was interrupted by a knock on the door bringing the family together to see who was there. A knock on their door always seemed to bring some sort of surprise. "Was it a visit from my future husband?" Andree hoped. "Maybe even a present from a relative?"

The door was opened and a tall, homely looking man stood in the doorway looking pensive and humble at the same time. He gently asked if Andree Laure Florin lived in the hillside villa. He spoke in an almost whisper as though afraid to upset someone.

"Yes," Auguste replied, and all eyes turned to Andree as she slowly came forward to show her face to the stranger.

The gentleman was carefully holding a package in his hands and, slowly, he began to unwrap it in front of her. Andree cried when she saw what he held. Then, with brokenness in his voice and a tear in his eyes, the kind gentleman asked, "Does this pocketbook belong to you?"

After six years, and what seemed like an eternity away, this man had found her lost but not forgotten white pocketbook stuffed with pictures and notes from Andree's youthful dreams. Among the ruins of their destroyed villa, this white purse with its shiny twin gold snaps stood out from all the wreckage. As the gentleman was cleaning up the debris, he recovered it and decided it might make one little girl very happy to have it back. Of course, he didn't know if she was still alive but this was a chance he wanted to take. If she hadn't survived the war, his visit could have brought the family painful memories that most villagers were trying to move beyond. He needed to take the chance when he fortunately discovered one piece of paper inside her pocketbook that had her name on it making it possible for the purse to be returned to its rightful owner.

Mom slipped into her room alone, wiped the tears from her eyes, and prepared herself for a momentous event. She knew life was a lot different than the last time she opened the white purse. She wondered if she even had the courage to unsnap the clips to look at what the inside of the purse might tell her about her life now, compared to her ambitions of yesteryear.

Eventually, she calmed herself down, took in one more deep breath, and unsnapped its golden clips. One by one, she pulled out pictures of friends. Some were still alive, while others she had not seen since the invasion. She read the notes slowly and painfully. Her emotions quickly overtook her again as she struggled at this crossroad of uncertainty. Finally, she put the pocketbook down and began to reason with her mixed emotions.

"Life is different now," she whispered through barely pursed lips. "I can't think of what might have been. I am to marry soon, although not anyone I knew growing up. I will leave my homeland and start a new life with a man I hadn't expected I'd be with, but I believe my husband will be a good man. He'll see to it that I am happy for the rest of my life. He is my hero."

Andree placed the notes and pictures back into the white pocketbook that was stained with colors of the debris of war and snapped it shut for the last time. She let go another deep breath, stood up, and placed the pocketbook up on her shelf for safekeeping. She then walked out into the room where her family waited for her to come out. Elizabeth looked at her daughter with tears in her own eyes too. She understood what had just happened to her daughter. She hugged Andree with both arms wrapped around her tightly, and neither one spoke a word.

Over the three years of their engagement, the correspondence with Andree's fiancé kept plans on track. Auguste wrote to Walter during the first part of the relationship, and eventually as was approved of by Auguste, Walter wrote directly to Andree.

Many times Mom doubted herself and whether she was or was not doing the right thing. She had to trust her parents and her own judgment and continue with the process that had progressed. Her other gentleman friend was angered that she had agreed to marry the American soldier, and when the American came to visit her one day, the two admirers ended up in a fist fight. The soldier won! He also won Andree's heart for keeps that day. I am very appreciative that things worked out that way or I would never have been here to write the story of how Andree Laure Florin and Sergeant Walter Warren Bannon met.

The final paperwork for marriage took seemingly forever to process. Mom had to prove that she was not a German woman. Then she had to prove she was healthy with no diseases, then a Catholic. Walter had to switch from being a Protestant to a Catholic, because the Catholic Church rules didn't allow marriage to another faith. This was not necessarily an easy switch for Walter coming from a New England Baptist family. The hurdles were numerous, but one by one, they were overcome. Finally, a wedding date was set, and on July 23rd, 1948, Andree L. Florin was married in a Catholic Church in Bouillon to her hero, Walter W. Bannon of East Hartford, Connecticut.

Mom was quite naive for twenty-two years old. Her dad had kept her on a short leash, so to speak. She didn't date, she'd never had a boyfriend, and she admitted that she didn't know what love was. She knew her father's love, and she knew about family love, but this would be a whole new experience.

The newlyweds set out together on their honeymoon to the Belgian coast and a beautiful resort village called LaPanne. Two lives from two different countries, seemingly worlds apart, became the foundation for a generation of six half French and half American children. This would be the start of not only a new life, but also a challenge completely unlike living through World War II.

Andree's first challenge came as a newlywed. Although she was now married to Walter, she wouldn't be able to live with him because of his obligations to the army in Germany. They remained separated for a few months while Walter completed his military commitments. Andree lived at home in Bouillon during this separation and confessed that it was hard for her to live apart from her husband. People gave her strange looks in the town as though she were having marital problems already.

Eventually, Walter received his new orders and was released from his tour of duty in the ETO (European Theatre of Operations). His new duty station would be stateside! The bride and groom prepared to head to New York City to begin their life together on America's soil where the real adventure would begin.

In my ongoing task of organizing boxes of pictures, books and old papers, I came across another interesting article that Mom had clipped out of the newspaper. It was headlined, *War Brides are Sought* (13). It told of the nearly one million war brides that returned to the United States after the war either as fiancées or wives. A couple of ladies from California were trying to assemble a list of two thousand war brides to write their life stories for a new book being published. They were also planning a reunion in 1985 on the Queen Mary ship now anchored proudly and permanently in California as a museum. I don't know that Mom ever contributed to the stories, but she always saved anything with relevance to her life's story. Finding this newspaper clipping was one more tug at my heart to discover how much it meant to her to retain pieces of her European life while she struggled to walk her American journey.

9. MY AMERICA

ndree, the naive little Walloon girl from Bouillon, was ready to embark on one huge adventure. The newlyweds boarded the majestic Queen Mary passenger ship and sailed out on their fourteen-day voyage across the Atlantic Ocean to the shores of America.   As they sailed out of Bremerhaven, Germany, they threw their coins down to the people below in a traditional gesture that they wouldn't need the Pfennigs and Francs in the new world. They were going to New York!

As Andree fantasized about the lovely and romantic voyage awaiting the new couple, she soon discovered that she had just entered a new war zone. Her accommodations once on board the ship were far from romantic.

As Walter and Andree stood in line to organize the passengers, the captain and crew directed all of the new wives and fiancées of soldiers into one very large room of the ship while the soldiers were all placed into another area of the ship. The separate quarters became their accommodations for the entire trip.

Mom recalled that it was a terrible trip for her because the French wives hated the German wives. She painfully remembered that they were always fighting and not just verbally. In order for Mom to avoid getting drawn into the conflict, she would find refuge by pulling the covers over her head and not saying a word. It's likely that she was the tiniest lady in the room, so her rehearsed ability to remain inconspicuous during Bouillon's occupation probably came in useful here as well.

Sailing into New York Harbor for the first time, Andree saw the Statue of Liberty proudly hoisting her flame of freedom. She recalled that the statue was a gift from France to America as a symbol of everlasting friendship. The broken chain that lies at the statue's feet as a symbol of freedom from the chains of oppression epitomized Mom's plight. Her chains had been broken also. The sight of the proud statue moved Mom to tears.

"I am free; I am truly free," she shouted to the new world.

Andree imagined that Lady Liberty quietly smiled back at her. She wished she could have hugged her the way she hugged the statue of Godfroi De Bouillon.

The mighty passenger ship that once ferried American soldiers to Europe to help liberate her touched the pier in New York without a quiver. Mom watched as the crew tied huge ropes to hold the giant ship in place. Its significance was not lost by Andree. At this location, so many of the tired and poor escaped the ravages of tyrants down through the ages, and now it was her turn. As she stepped off of the floating city and onto land, Mom felt the true meaning of being free beating in her heart. Years later, she still could not describe the emotion she felt.

Andree's new surroundings posed unique new problems that often, would end up getting her into awkward situations. For example, immediately after arriving in New York, the young couple was staying at a lovely hotel. Wanting to experience an indoor pool for the first time, Andree asked the receptionist where the pool was, albeit speaking in French. Now in French, the word for pool is *piscine*, pronounced, *pissin*. The hotel staff pointed to a ladies bathroom down the hallway thinking she needed to use it, but Mom just walked past the bathroom and proceeded down the hall to the swimming pool room. She waded into the nice warm water and with a look of relief on her face, looked back, waved, and smiled at the kind receptionist. She got a few repulsive glares from that poor young lady who became concerned about the hygiene within the pool area. This experience would define the rest of Andree's life, learning to be an American wife. Mom, the Walloon war bride, just took one day at a time learning and adapting to a new way of life in this big new world called The Unites States of America.

For Andree, the move from Bouillon to New York was a major adjustment. Mom had hardly ever been out of her birthplace home, and now she was in New York City. It was such a busy place and there were so many cars. She and Dad lived in an Army-supplied trailer on an Army post just outside of New York City, beneath the George Washington Bridge. The enclave was called Fort Jay. The trailer they lived in was a very small home. It measured on about eighteen feet long and perhaps ten feet wide. It barely had enough room for the small black and white television set they owned. Color TV had not yet been invented.

Andree was not too thrilled with the accommodations. Her new home left much to be desired in comparison with her homes and villa she'd had growing up. She still tried to be positive about the direction of her new life with her husband. At least it was immeasurably better than her accommodations for four years under Nazi control.

Walter's sister lived in a small fishing village in Connecticut called Noank. It was located about a two-hour drive North on Route One. As often as they could, they would visit his sister and brother-in-law there. Mom loved the smell of the salt water of Long Island Sound and talked about someday moving there. They saw a few cute homes had come up for sale, but the young newlyweds had very little money put aside to make her dream affordable.

During the two years living in New York, Andree gave birth to two daughters, Marian Monique, born August 3rd, 1949, and Elaine Elizabeth, born July 30th, 1950. It was a tight fit in the tin-can trailer as the babies had to sleep in a dresser drawer, but that was short lived because Dad was re-assigned by the army back to France. Walter and Andree with their two daughters would end up taking a ten day trip from New York across the Atlantic Ocean to Germany aboard The USS Patch. This ship was another huge passenger liner similar to The Queen Mary.

While in France, Mom had her first son, Christian Emile, born on October 6th, 1952. Due to a problem with hospital overcrowding in France, he was born in Landsthul, Germany, not far from the border. "Did this make her first son a German citizen," she wondered?

In America, if you are born here, you are an American with all of the protections of an American citizen. Chris had to affirm his American citizenship when he enlisted in the U.S. Army effectively having to choose to relinquish any citizenship claims to Germany.

In 1954, Andree had another daughter. Phyllis Eloise was born in France on June 29th. Three beautiful girls and one boy were now part of this growing concern. Unfortunately, the Army again moved the family. This time, they were relocated to New London, Connecticut. Now they were only about ten miles from where Walter's family lived in Noank. Mom rejoiced to know that she would be near family. She knew that she needed support with Walter being gone so much on his military travels and didn't feel as alone with the in-laws living nearby. His constant absence was typical of soldiers who often get transferred from base to base. Sometimes they could take their families with them, and sometimes they couldn't.

It was during this relocation process that Mom faced what would become one of her worst American nightmares. Post WWII United States was moving to a dangerous precipice with respect to accusing and suspecting fellow Americans of supporting Communism. Senator Joseph McCarthy, a one-time candidate for the presidency, pushed for stricter laws to defend against potential secret Communist infiltrators. Companies were scanned for illegal activities and, in a dark time for this country, many citizens became involved in a "witch-hunt" for Communists. McCarthy even stated that there were Communists in the American government. This caused a lot of people to dislike him as it put many patriotic Americans on edge.

Mom, Dad, and the four children landed in New York during the height of this mania. Because she was French, and erroneously thought to look like a spy with her shifting eyes, she was immediately taken away from her children and placed into a holding area. The patrol agents suspected that she might be a communist infiltrator. Mom was infuriated at being incarcerated.

The children were allowed to leave, so Walter took them to live with the in-laws in Noank while he tried to work out the details of her hopeful release.

"How could this be happening?" Andree wondered.

Mom had always played by the rules, and now, the country that saved her life and that she loved so much had placed her in confinement. This brought back painful memories of the restricted living during the occupation of Belgium. Mom remained interred for days, wondering if she would lose her four children. Word spread and rumors flew that she would have to return to Belgium alone. She couldn't have been more insulted over the thought that she was not a patriot. She loved America!

"Can't somebody help me?" she cried.

At only twenty-eight years old, having survived World War II, she realized that she was still all too vulnerable. She wondered if Auguste, her father, could help her as he had done during the occupation, but she had no means to contact him other than by a letter. She knew this would take too long to get results so her only possible hope rested in Walter's efforts and prayer. Walter feverishly transported documents through the war department and local military bases pleading for help but some officials told him he might need to plead his case to higher authorities.

Mom told me that because of this event, Senator Joe McCarthy was the third man on her list of the three men that she hated. "He did this to me," Mom said. "First it was Adolph Hitler, who destroyed my home. Then Leon Degrelle became a traitor who brought the Nazi's wrath to our town. Then Senator McCarthy put me into jail."

McCarthy was number three. This was the circle of enemies that she stated, "Ruined my life."

On the fourth day of her confinement, Walter arrived to meet with her and discuss her options. He had met with some of the highest people in command at the local military bases and managed to get paperwork stating that she should be released. Their requirement would be that she would agree to become a citizen of the United States. That was an easy decision for her. It was a done deal!

After this settlement Mom was released from internment and returned to her family. In 1956, she officially became an American citizen never again to be denied her rights to live free of oppression. Once again, the military came to her rescue. It is no wonder that throughout her lifetime Mom has held such high regard for military men and women. She owed her life to the military from the day they entered Bouillon to set the town free, to the daily living accommodations they provided, and for being set free from the snares of an out of control, anti-communist Senator.

"Thank God for the Army!" Mom often states. "God Bless America!" is another refrain I regularly hear from her.

She always states these pronouncements with a smile and enthusiasm. If she hears anyone else speak those hallowed words, they too will find a warm smile returned to them.

Walter was happy to be re-assigned to New London, Connecticut, to fill a recruiting spot. The good news was that now they would be close to Noank, that pretty little fishing village up the coast of Connecticut. Mom encouraged Walter to seek out a home there for them.

One day when they were visiting with Walter's sister, Andree looked out the kitchen window and saw a small home up on the hill. She commented about how she liked it, and her sister in law said that she knew the owners and knew that they were interested in selling it. After some back and forth offers and some paperwork, in 1955, Walter and Andree bought their first home. "I will never move again," proclaimed Andree, who now felt the joy of staking a claim to a piece of American soil.

Noank was the same charming village where Emelia Earhart was married to George Putnam. Emelia was the pilot who became famous for being the first woman to fly around the world. Unfortunately, it is presumed that she crashed her plane on a remote island in the South Pacific and never completed the trip. I discovered in Mom's many boxes, an envelope in which she had saved the news clipping of the story about Emelia's wedding.

Noank was a beautiful area to settle down and raise a family and Walter and Andree were well into that part of the task. They paid nine thousand dollars for the little house that perched on top of Prospect Hill. This was the first commitment to settling down that they had made since their marriage. The house needed a lot of work, but that didn't matter. The upstairs of the home was one large attic where Mom hung blankets from the ceilings to create the effect of separate bedrooms.

On July 3rd in 1955, Walter Warren Jr. was born close by, in Groton, Connecticut, on the Naval Submarine Base. This would be a place where Mom would spend a lot of days. The large Navy base had grocery stores and shops that were all discounted for their military families. There was a theatre and a *piscine* there along with so many opportunities to keep her children busy. It was the perfect place for the stable settled life she had always wanted. At least it was perfect until 1957, when Walter was re-assigned to Germany. Sadly, Andree would have to leave her home but, instead of selling the house, Mom convinced Dad to just rent it out. She vowed to return to this home that she loved so dearly.

Walter and Andree loaded the entire family, two adults and five children, and loads of baggage, into a C-130 cargo jet and flew to Frankfurt, Germany. The trip back to Europe was by space available transport. The family sat on benches that were lined along the length of the plane, not facing forward but facing each other across the plane's belly. It was very loud. Everyone had to wear headphones to quiet down the loud drone of engine noise. Our travel accommodations were always what the military called "space available." When it came to flying, the whole family had to wait for a plane with enough empty room to fit all the children. Sometimes it meant waiting at the airport overnight until we got told to grab our bags and run. Dad would be required to go ahead of us, while we waited for days to get a flight since he usually had a reporting date at his new duty station.

The Bannon family lived in France with their cousins while Walter worked at his duty station nearby. I personally have very few memories of France at this early age. I did start to learn to speak a little bit of French however, and I recall the funny way the local children spoke to my mom. "Madame Banno," they called out. It must have been fun for them to pronounce that funny Irish name that translated meant banana, in the all-French speaking village!

On October 31st, 1957, Michael Stanley was born in Germany. He was the sixth child born to Mom. This was a big family, and not what she originally expected. She says that she never wanted to have children because of the memories of what she saw as the war's impact on children, but being Catholics, they couldn't use birth control according to church rules. Still, she loved each of her children with no regrets.

Michael was especially difficult in pregnancy. One day when her mother was visiting, Grandma told Andree that she didn't look very good. Agreeing that she'd felt sick for a while now, she went to the hospital in France. There, the doctors told her that there was no sign of life from her baby. This just wasn't acceptable. She refused to accept that report and cried, "No, my baby is okay. God will be with him!" She demanded that they check again and, upon further review, found a heartbeat. Mom decided, after that incident, to name her third son, Michael, after Michael the Archangel.

It was no surprise that Mom would not accept this report of losing her sixth child. She seemed to have a connection unlike any ever seen. I figured that maybe God had said to her, "Andree, you've lived a hard life, but you've been faithful. Whatever you want, I'll do it for you."

I know this sounds crazy, but recently I was driving with her in her car and I said, "Mom, it's going to be a rough drive with rain pouring down all the way to Connecticut."

With black clouds overhead, and downpours all around, she looked at me and said, "No, the weather will be sunny for us!"

Then like the heavens were granting her wish, the sun shined on us for the rest of the trip. These types of occurrences happened so many times that I stopped doubting her and decided I had better go along with her. Since she was that well connected to "The Boss," I didn't ever want to be on the opposing side.

In yet another event that reinforced my belief that she, like her dad, had a keen spiritual intuitiveness, this next episode so challenged me that I began to ponder my own standing.

I had joined the US Army when I was seventeen and I had experienced a very bad night at my army base in New Jersey during which I thought I might die from a drug overdose. After surviving the night, the next day I headed home for some serious recovery time and soul searching. Driving home on Interstate 95, about fifty miles from Noank, I got a flat tire on my old Ford Mustang. With no money in my wallet and no spare tire to replace the flat with, I looked up and complained, "What next?"

Frustrated at my streak of bad luck, I stuck my thumb out to hitch a ride and to my shock, the first car to pull over was driven by Mom. Wow! I was shocked. "What are you doing driving way out here?" I asked. I was awed at how her timing managed to intersect perfectly with my car's breakdown. She told me that she had decided to drive to Hartford to visit another brother-in-law that morning. I felt it couldn't have been a mere coincidence that she was there for me.

In the car she told me that on the night before, she was awakened by what seemed like a mysterious person sitting on the end of her bed. She took it as a sign that one of her kids was in trouble and needed her help, so she prayed all night for all of her children. Again, I was amazed! What could I say?

"It was me," I told her.

She had already figured that out when she saw me hitch-hiking on the highway looking all forlorn. After this experience I became more convinced that Mom marched to the beat of a heavenly drummer and I began a personal quest to get to know this drummer better.

Shortly after Mom's sixth child was born, Walter was re-assigned one more time. It would be back to Connecticut to finish a short-term position, after which he could finally retire. Once again, the whole family, six children with Mom and Dad, loaded into the passenger ship, USS Patch. It was another long trip across the Atlantic Ocean for Mom. I can't imagine how she managed to keep us all safe on that ship. She towed along three sons and three daughters and a room full of baggage! All her children had a similar independent spirit which made keeping track of us very challenging.

I remember how the ship would pitch from front to back ever so slowly. They warned us not to drink too much liquid because it would make you sick when the liquids in your stomach pitched slowly back and forth. It's not pretty but true, that there often were piles of vomit in the hallways where others had become sea sick. One day my brother and I were running through the hallways and he slipped in one of the piles. I thought it was so funny that I laughed till I cried. On another night, I was sleeping in the top bunk and my little brother was in the bottom bunk. I began to feel sick and leaned over the edge of the bed to throw-up. Just then I saw my little brothers face laying over the edge of his bed. I thought for a minute how funny it would be to splash him, but at the last second, in a moment of brotherly kindness, I redirected my sickness away from his head. He never even woke up. I told him about it the next day though.

Mom was valiant, like Godfroi, to be able to endure raising these six children, and so often on her own. She had many ups and downs, including losing her youngest daughter to cancer in 1983. Phyllis had married and had one son, but during the pregnancy of her second son, she developed breast cancer. Not wanting to hurt her second son, she refused to take any chemical therapy. Unfortunately, after giving birth to her second son, her cancer grew to a non-reversible point. Phyllis came back to Connecticut to live with Mom for a time, but in the end, she lost her battle. The loss hurt Mom deeply, and brought her to depths of pain she had not known before. She calls losing her youngest daughter one of her greatest heartaches. Like Auguste, she did all she could for Phyllis, and like the war, some battles were won and some were lost.

Mom smiles when we tell her that she'll she Phyllis again. She'll see a lot of people again. I'm not the judge of where she'll see them, but I think she'll be hanging around with the likes of Mother Teresa and other special ladies of history who've impacted many but never received any special recognition. Mom may not be in any book of Who's Who in America, but she'll always be number one in my book of heroes.

10. THE AMERICAN HERO

Walter didn't talk to his children very much about his time in the army or about what his role was in France and Belgium. He did once tell me that he held a top-secret security clearance and, for a short time, he worked for the U.N. in New York. He said that he was a personal chauffer for General Dwight D. Eisenhower. This same general became the 34th President of the United States in 1953. Eisenhower was also largely credited with the successful war strategy to help defeat Hitler. I remember growing up thinking, "My dad must be an important man!" I reasoned that this was why he didn't tell us much about his life. He had important secrets to keep.

I also imagined it was why he was gone from home so much. I missed not having him home when I was a young boy, then as a high school student. Seeing this lifestyle's impact on our family, I vowed not to be a father in absentia when I had kids.

Dad had a scar on his knee. He said it was a bullet wound. I never did get confirmation on that or whether he was just pulling my leg when I would ask him about it. I accepted the war wound explanation and added it to one of the few personal things I knew about Dad. Later in life I noticed that he walked with a limp on that same bullet scarred side. Often, he stood slightly tilted to favor that leg. Again, I accepted this as one of his war injuries.

Dad did share with me one event about when his expert shooting came in useful in the march to free Belgium. He explained that his platoon was marching in rank and file up the dirt roads littered with battle wreckage heading towards Hitler's retreating armies, when he was called to come to the front of the platoon. There, he was told that the forward spotters had located a German sniper hiding in a tree. Knowing that Walter could shoot highly accurate, they had him get as close to the target as possible, and then take one shot at the hand that was holding the sniper in the tree. The rest of the sniper's figure was well hidden. It was critical for this sniper to be taken out of commission so that the platoon could move on.

With Walter's calm hand and a powerful scope mounted on his M1 bolt action rifle, he set the Nazi's hand at the center of the scope's crosshairs, took a deep breath, calmly exhaled, then squeezed off one round. It was a perfect shot, knocking the sniper from the tree and onto the ground. I asked him what became of the sniper, and he said that the other troops took care of him once he was on the ground. I believe that Dad did his job, but did not glory in having to assist with killing an enemy combatant. Far too many of the Axis soldiers were mere boys brainwashed or forced into fighting a war they neither started nor believed in.

Walter was always the military man. It was whom he was from start to finish. Some of my most fond memories of Dad were seeing him marching in the Memorial Day parades in Noank. One year, he even led the parade in full uniform. He proudly wore his decorations from World War II and many other awards from his long and faithful service in the military. He served in Korea for a short time and had a pin for that too. He had a pin for being an expert rifleman and a pin for being a recruiter. I recall watching him clean and polish each medal, one at a time, before a parade. In his last year of military service, he received a commission to Lieutenant Colonel. He received this commission after twenty-seven years of what the army calls a hard-striper. This promotion to an officer's rank is awarded after many years doing everything required from the E-1 to E-9 rank. He especially loved those two new silver leaf clusters on his shoulders. This not only gave him a good retirement pay, it also meant that every other uniformed serviceman was required to salute him in respect for his grade. It is a mutually appreciated act of respect for all military men and women.

I learned very early on in my army career that only officers were to be saluted. If a young recruit saluted a drill sergeant, which they often did just out of fear, the recruit would usually get yelled at. "I'm not an officer, soldier, I work for a living," the sergeant would yell. Often, this led to new soldiers being punished with having to perform pushups or stand at attention for an hour. In fact I managed to get yelled at a few times during my three years in the army.

Dad was very proud of the fact that four of his children served in the military. I was the third to enlist in the army, after Chris and Marian. I started my basic training at Fort Dix, New Jersey. I was very green about many things having grown up in a small rural fishing village with a Belgian mother. I'll never forget how unprepared I was for being thrust into this environment.

On day one of basic training, they sat us all in chairs for haircuts first. I had shoulder length hair after high school. The sergeant asked me how I wanted my hair, then proceeded to cut it all off and hand it to me saying, "Is this how you wanted it?" I wasn't amused. My recruiter had told me that this was a new army and that we would have more rights! "Where were mine?" I wondered.

After our humiliating haircuts, the staff took all of my civilian clothes away, gave me green clothing and white underwear in a duffle bag, lined me up with fifty other brutal looking guys for a bunch of shots, showed us our bunks to sleep on, and told us to start cleaning the floors. It was the weekend, and I thought that we had weekends off! Oh well, I was disappointed, but I had to get through this for Dad.

The next morning, I began to sort through all the clothing I was given. Growing up the French boy, I had never seen these white boxers before. My mom always bought us French styled briefs. It was Sunday morning and I wanted to go out running since I was a cross-country runner in high school. I pulled out the boxers and slipped one on. Wow, it had a flimsy fly in the front, and they were quite thin, so I slipped another one on in the same direction. Now with two pairs of boxers on, they didn't seem too bad to use for jogging shorts. I bolted out the front door of our barracks, bald headed, with a white t-shirt and two pairs of boxers on, wearing army green socks and very heavy army boots for running shoes. It was nothing like wearing my high school track uniform, but it was okay for now.

What I didn't know was that this was also the weekend for parents to come and visit the soldiers that were graduating after months of hard training. The parents were all dressed so formal. There were officers and enlisted men everywhere. As I ran over the sidewalks and along the streets around the base, I saw mothers and fathers smiling at me. Some waved and I waved back, and some looked away. I figured they were all happy to see me running so hard.

As I neared the barracks, I heard my name being yelled out. "Bannon, get over here!" It was my drill sergeant with some of the other new recruits standing next to him. I recognized his voice from the night before but wondered why he would be yelling at me so loud for training on a weekend.

"He should be pleased," I thought.

When I got to the door of our barracks, my drill sergeant proceeded to embarrass me in front of my fellow troops, yelling at me for running around "his" army base in my underwear, especially on family visitation weekend. He had me stand there at attention, while he verbally assaulted me. He said, "If you ever dress like that in public again, I will take that can filled with cigarette butts and shove it up your ^%$*^."

I tried to explain that I had a French mother who never bought us boxers, and that I wore two pairs for modesty, but he would take no explanations.

He sent me in to get dressed and to do kitchen duty for the rest of the weekend. That meant peeling potatoes for the staff, then washing dishes. I hated washing dishes! I guess I made quite a first impression at that army base. I never did tell Dad about that incident.

Another memory I have of my father was of him practicing shooting his rifles and his German Lugar in our backyard in Noank. I was extremely excited that he allowed me to shoot his rifle once. He loved guns, especially if they were of World War II significance. He was very fond of his German Lugar with all matching low numbers on it. He respectfully told me that it came from a dead Nazi soldier. I don't think Mom liked his guns at all. They reminded her of the gunfire she heard during the war. She always hoped he would sell them, but she wouldn't ever win that battle.

Walter was a gifted piano player. He didn't read music but could play most anything by ear including harmonica and accordion. Sometimes we would sit around the piano and sing songs with our company. He loved to play for visitors in our house. If we went out anywhere, and there happened to be a piano in the establishment, he would always get permission to play it. He loved to draw a crowd, and he usually did that with joy, taking requests and getting perfect strangers to sing along. Before he died, he had been volunteering to play music in the Catholic Church in Gales Ferry, just outside of the Navy base in Groton. Mom recently told me that Dad also loved Irish songs. I never knew that.

Dad purchased a boat when he finally settled into his last job in New London. We used to ride in it to Mystic and Stonington. Sometimes we would go fishing for flounder or just sleep overnight in the cabin. It was a great experience for about one or two years in the summer. It always made me feel proud to see him as captain of his ship.

Dad also loved to roller skate, so he would volunteer to drive the Mystic Community Center's bus trips to Warwick, Rhode Island, on the weekends. I enjoyed these trips also. Mom usually stayed home alone. Unfortunately, our family experiences with him could be assembled on just a few lines. I always ached for a deeper relationship with him.

Sadly, it wasn't until I had completed my tour in Germany that Dad and I looked at each other on the same level. It was then that my relationship changed from being a child to becoming best friends. I seemed to have gained his respect and it was time to start to build our friendship.

Unfortunately, it was not going to be easy. I had started a life of my own. I had my own apartment, my own friends, my own music, and eventually, in 1980, I married Marilea Copp, of New London, and we moved to Maine to work in the cable television industry. Our bonding opportunities would be brief after that. Dad died in 1994 from a heart attack at his home in Connecticut.

It's interesting that Leon Degrelle died in the same year that Dad died. These two men, who impacted Andree's life in diametrically opposite ways, lived across the globe from each other but found release from this world at almost the same time.

At Dad's funeral, I grieved most for the missed opportunities a father and son could have had. He was my hero, too, and I will always remember him as such! Two letters I found in Mom's boxes drew my interest from their blank envelopes. I pulled them out and wept as I read the words that sadly reinforced the heartaches of my youth. One of them read,

> *Dear DaDDy, We hope ThaT you come Back soon. We will Be very happy when you come. We are waiting very paChonlee for you. I am going To make my communion. When you come back. We all still*

love you a loTe we realy care for you very much. Love Wally Bannon

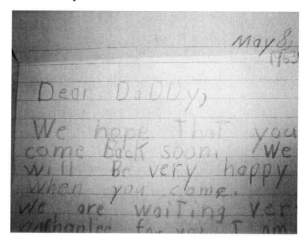

The other letter was a similar appeal for him to please come home for Easter.

Dad spent his final years riding motorcycles, going to parades, and doing the things he loved to do. In 1986 he purchased a new motorcycle and took Mom on a cross-country ride to Tulsa, Oklahoma to visit Marian.

Dad never quit being a soldier. It was his number one priority in life. The military owned him, and he was never willing to bend his commitment to the United States Army. Mom loved her hero, and her hero loved the army. He was the consummate soldier, faithful to the end.

11. GROWING UP FRENCHIE

L ife wasn't always easy growing up as the little French boy. I used to get laughed at in school because I didn't know how to pronounce certain words that most children could handle at my age. Words like scissors, I pronounced, *see zos*, because that's how Mom pronounced them. This sometimes got schoolmates asking me to speak difficult words for their friends. Oh yes, I was quite the source for a good laugh. As children, we did the same with Mom and her mispronunciations. We would ask her to say refrigerator or linoleum just to get a laugh from our friends. Mom always obliged and laughed along with us. She still today can't say these words in English without drawing a chuckle from the listener.

A good example of my poor communication abilities came one day when I was sitting at my school desk. I needed to use the bathroom so bad that my back teeth were floating. I did everything right, I thought. I raised my hand, and then I asked the teacher if I could go to the bathroom. She asked me, "Is it an emergency?"

I always thought that an emergency meant that someone needed an ambulance. Consequently, I said, "No."

About two minutes later, I couldn't hold back the river any longer, and I just let it flow. Of course, I was as discreet as possible. I just soaked my shorts and then sat there like nothing had happened.

I don't know if it was time to go out to play, or if the teacher just thought it was beginning to smell bad in my corner, but the rest of the class was let out to go to recess. After they left, my teacher asked me why I had not told her how bad I had to go. I reminded her that she asked me if it was an emergency, and that an emergency meant ambulances to me. I put the blame squarely on her shoulders. "I guess I taught her a lesson," I thought.

Unimpressed, she then sent me home to change my clothes. Mom was surprised but knew I had communication difficulties just like her. We lived right next to the school, so it was convenient at times like this. Unfortunately, our proximity to the school opened the door for activities of a mischievous nature also.

One such event took place on the school roof. Being a good climber, and always wanting a better perspective of the playground, I found a succession of ledges and window trims that gave me just enough grab handles to get up onto the top of the tall school roof. What a view I had from up there. I used the advantage of height to hurl down stones at my friends below in an after-school game of war. They'd throw rocks at me, and I would throw handfuls of roof-stone at them. After an hour of war, I had managed to cover the entire school playground with thousands of little rocks.

The next day at school, I was called into the principal's office. They knew that I lived next door, and they knew I had a mischievous tendency with an uncanny ability to climb, being as I was so light and nimble. I was the obvious perpetrator of this early childhood crime. Mom was disappointed with me, but without a father at home to role model I was always testing the limits of my mother's patience. My climbing abilities carried over to some other tomfoolery in my community where I was known to climb telephone poles in a game of hide and seek with the local police. After I got out of the army, I ended up climbing telephone poles as a cable television technician for a career. I guess I was just continuing to use of my natural born talents.

Another school episode would find my older brother, Chris, and I using the school's high overhead bars for a jumping off point in an effort to glide through the air. It seems that my brother's obsession with flying didn't end with the broken arm he got from jumping off of a stone wall with a Superman cape tied around his neck. He needed more challenges, and since I was such a gullible younger brother, I would be a good assistant for his tests.

First, he explained to me that if we each stood up on the high bars with a grip on the edges of this large plastic bag, then when we jumped off, we should gently float to the ground like those parachute jumpers. I believed him, and we tried it. Like the Wright brothers who failed before they succeeded, we also failed. We crashed to the ground with a thud and I gained a fat lip. It seems that we couldn't hold the plastic bag in our hands due to the air resistance. Maybe we should have tried tying the bag to our hands so that we couldn't let go?

Not to be defeated, Chris calculated that a four by eight sheet of plywood held over his head would serve as a glide if he could get high enough for the wind to catch it. That's when we devised a plan to get a plywood sheet up on the school roof. I wasn't going to be the first one to test this theory though. Once on the roof, Chris lifted the huge board over his head with his arms spread across the four-foot span. I was ready to witness his flight and measure its success from the ground below. "One, two, three, jump," I shouted.

He leapt off the roof and, immediately, I realized that this was a bad idea. The board flipped up vertically, and both Chris and the board crash-landed just about three feet away from the school. The only injuries he incurred were where the board had hit him on the head, and he'd gotten a small bruise in his pride.

One year, Chris built a tree fort very high up in a tree and invited me up to see it. I was very impressed, but there was no way I was going to attempt any of his new glider tricks from this height. I decided to leave the fort, stepping down the many nailed boards to get to the bottom. I suddenly felt rain falling on my head. Looking up, I realized that it wasn't rain falling on me. Rain isn't typically yellow. I guess it was just an act of sibling play, but as Mom walked down the road and saw what was happening, she yelled up to Chris, "What are you doing?"

He replied, "I'm just watering the plants!"

I gave up following his ideas of flight after that, but Chris went on to avionics school in Georgia and even did some parachute jumps in the Army. He was in Thailand for a while and then was stationed in Hawaii for two more years.

Now, I had a younger brother who in turn became the recipient of my experiments too. I loved to create electronic things even though I didn't know anything about electronics. One day, I decided to trick my little brother, Mikey, into believing that I had built a robot. I took a cardboard box and stuck radio tubes all over it. Then I put lights and wires coming out all over the place. I took an iron from Mom's ironing table and placed it underneath the robot. With the robot plugged into the wall, and the iron adjustment set for steam, I told my brother to reach underneath the robot to see if it was over-heating.

"Ouch, it's over-heating," he cried.

Mike was impressed that I had built a working robot, and aside from a couple of burned fingers, he was okay. I tried some of those other funny experiments on him that Chris tried on me. I was just a little bit more malicious to him than Chris was to me, but that was simply the pecking order of sibling rivalry taking its natural course.

Mike survived all of my tricks. I just don't know who he could test his tricks on, being the youngest one in the family. He joined the Army and studied helicopter maintenance, even going to Saudi Arabia after the first Gulf War to wrap up helicopters to bring home after the conflict.

My passion for electronics included a basement full of junk televisions and radios. I wanted to fix them up, but again, I knew little about how to do these repairs. I changed tubes, tapped here and there and, once in a while, I succeeded in getting something working again. Our basement in Noank was always flooded, and sometimes it had up to six inches of water in it. This was a dangerous arrangement when working with electronic gear. One day I was watching the high voltage blue arc on the inside of a television set. It could be very dangerous to touch. I was standing on a damp floor, and

I attempted to move the arc around with a screwdriver. I thought that the rubber handle insulated me, but I quickly discovered that 20,000 volts would jump a long way to get to a ground. Consequently, the arc jumped from the television to my finger and from my toe to the wet floor. The shock knocked me back against the wall almost killing me. After that episode, Mom decided it was time to enroll me into electronics school in Norwich, Connecticut.

It was at the vocational school that I discovered an ability to run fast and far. I joined the cross-country team, and since it was a trade school with few girls, we didn't have any cheerleaders. Mom thought this was unfortunate so she became the cheerleader. She and my sister, Phyllis, got pom-poms with the school's colors and cheered us on at all of our races. During my last two years in high school, I won the Quinnebaug Valley Conference Division three-mile race title. Just like Mom's physical stature, I only had about ninety-five pounds of body weight to carry around, so it was easy for me to run against guys who were sometimes two or three times my size. Mom told me after I had won that big race that she had prayed for me. It again made me consider her connections, because she always seemed to get what she asked for. I honestly was shocked to have won the title, but I always attributed it to Mom's prayers.

If Mom didn't have enough trials with being alone so often, and trying to raise six kids while working as a house cleaner to earn extra money to pay the bills, I think my sea-going adventures may have provided her some extra troubles and gray hairs.

Living in the coastal community of Noank, I loved to fish and go out on boats. I also loved to swim in the salt water off of the town pier. Sometimes my friends and I would watch a sailboat approach, and then in a mad stroke, swim fast enough to grab hold of the dinghy that trailed behind. Once our free ride approached the marina that was about a three minute ride along the shore, we would let go and either swim back or grab a return dinghy. I don't think the sailboat captains appreciated it, but it was pretty harmless mischief from our perspective.

Mom's gray hairs were added to on another one of my boating adventures with a buddy. He and I decided to take his small rowboat out across Fishers Island Sound from his dock in Noank. The trip was about six miles to Fishers Island, which is part of New York. Unfortunately, the boat only had a five-horse engine on it. This was hardly sufficient for a trip this far. The ride would take us well over two hours. We left Noank at two o clock in the afternoon, with no planning. We had no shirts and no shoes, just bathing suits and a boat. This trip would take us across the protected Long Island Sound, but this area is also known for its strong currents between tides. On a prior sailing adventure when I was only thirteen I had to be rescued in a tiny ten-foot sailboat that had a broken centerboard, causing us to drift from the sheltered sound out into the wild blue sea. Fortunately, before dusk, we were spotted by perhaps the last sailboat heading into the Mystic River that night. They thankfully towed us back to Noank.

On the Fishers Island excursion however, the weather was a bit rough for the small rowboat we were in. We made it to the island by about 4:30 pm but, by then, we were cold and tired. We had no food and no money and were not particularly looking forward to getting back into the boat for another rough two or three hour trip home. Knowing that we were both supposed to be at our dishwashing jobs in Noank by 6:00 pm, we called our employer from a payphone we found on the island. We explained to the operator that we had no money and convinced her to put the call through to the restaurant. Once we were connected, we left a message with an employee that we were on Fishers Island, and we didn't know if we would make it back for work. We probably should have re-phrased that to say, "We might not try to come back for work because it was getting rough on the ocean."

After the call, my friend and I proceeded to walk around the island searching out an answer to our predicament. After a couple more hours of wandering around on this seemingly deserted island, we started thinking of survival options. We were cold, hungry, and tired.

Our plans decidedly changed from heading back, to hunkering down somewhere in a building or a shed. We looked for clothing on clotheslines but didn't find any. We walked the seemingly endless dirt roads in hopes of finding a store, but there was nothing open. I was beginning to wonder why we hadn't planned our trip better than this. I trusted my friend's boating skills, but I knew very little about his judgment.

Back at home, Mom hadn't heard from me and called my friend's home only to find out that we had headed out in a rowboat almost six hours earlier. She decided to check in at our restaurant to see if they had heard from us. It was then that her biggest fears were realized. The people at work told her that we had called in from the island and reported that, "We might not make it back." The translation was lacking clarity.

Mom headed to the shore where we'd left from, and there, both families started calling for us and shining flashlights out into the ocean. The search was on. The U.S. Coast Guard was notified of a missing boat in Long Island Sound with two young boys aboard. From Westerly, Rhode Island, to New Haven, Connecticut, search boats were sent out to find us.

Back on the island, we were exhausted. Our bare feet were getting blistered as we continued to walk in search of a refuge. My friend told me about a lighthouse that he could see from his home at night that shined from the far end of the island. He said that there was a Coast Guard station there, and that it might be occupied. Even though we were both almost too tired to go on, we decided to head for the tip of the Island. At this point, we could think of no other option. It was around nine-o-clock in the evening, when a lone car drove up alongside of us and asked me who I was. "Walt Bannon," I replied.

The man was driving a car that was marked U.S. Coast Guard on the side. In a fairly irate tone of voice, he began to tell us that the whole Eastern Coast of Connecticut was looking for us. He told us to get in the car and said that he would drive us to the station. He grabbed his walkie-talkie and reported to the station that two lost boys fitting the right descriptions were just located about one mile from the island's tip. Then the gentleman calmed down and asked us if we were hungry. He saw that we were shivering and tired and said that we could sleep at the station. He told us that we would be allowed to head back to Noank the next day.

At the station, my friend and I were given shirts to wear that read U.S. Coast Guard. The gentleman gave us some warm soup, and then we were handed a telephone. He suggested we call home first. He said that we had some pretty nervous parents waiting for a call. When I got through to Mom, she was delirious with joy that we were okay. I told her what had happened, and while I should have been scolded, she was just happy that we were alive.

The gentleman then showed us our beds. We were both too tired to do anything else but sleep, even though we were offered a movie to watch. I thought that it was pretty cool that we were sleeping in the Coast Guard Station. In the morning we got eggs and bacon and got to watch television and look at all of their charts. I really liked this part of our trip!

After a quick lesson on the hazards of the ocean we took a short ride back to our boat sitting lonely on the banks of the southern tip of the island. We boarded our undersized vessel and began the long trip home. It gave us plenty of time to think about our error-filled journey. We also knew that we were going to hear it from our parents. The Coast Guardsmen watched from shore as we motored away through a calm mid-tide sea.

On the shore in Noank, there was a small group of family and friends that had gathered. It was like a homecoming event, but one that should never have happened. I didn't smile too much as we approached within view of our reception group. We knew there would be as much consternation as there was joy, so we just made our way to shore and hugged our mothers.

I put Mom through many other difficulties over the years. Now I look back and realize how foolish some of my adventures were. I was an entrepreneur even at the earliest of years. In school, I often walked to town on lunch breaks, with orders for chewing gum from the students. I could make a nickel a stick, and that profit would pay for my own candy. Later, I got into trouble for selling fireworks. I caused Mom a serious embarrassment that day when she had to ride in a police car to pick me out of the Noank crowd I hung with. I always had to be creative because I had very little money to buy things with, but my entrepreneurial ventures often got me into trouble.

The struggle to keep us out of mischief was relayed to a distant husband by Andree. I found letters that Mom sent to Dad asking how she could possibly be expected to manage alone. Her anger rose when she faced the reality that he was away to another war zone. This time he was in Korea, and she was left with six kids and little money. The broken down car and the bills were an ever-present source of anxiety for Mom. Dad seemed to always push the bills further and further down the road. He'd refinance the house and do whatever it took to get the toys he wanted, but paying down debt was not his priority.

Dad always had the military and, I think because of that, he wasn't forced to make the wise financial decisions that would have helped make our lives much better. Mom never said anything to us growing up but, deep inside her heart, it must have been unbearable to learn that her hero was fallible and that the perfect man that rescued her from the terrible grip of Hitler's armies had left her in the grip of a life of uncertainty and pain. She kept it all to herself, barely showing her grief. I think that she always looked for the next rainbow over the next storm cloud.

Mom learned to look beyond the pain and see the future as a bright place. I know this is what kept her going. She would never give up, and she would never surrender. It's who she was and who she is. It was her dream to be happy, and she was going to be happy no matter how difficult circumstances could be at times.

12. BANNON FAMILY SINGERS

Mom had a lot to be worried about trying to raise three boys and three girls, but she also had a lot to be proud of. Although her children tested her in every way possible, the flip side to the coin was the public recognition she received when her children excelled in academics, music, or some type of sports competition.

With Dad's musical talent beginning to flow down and through the veins of his children, Mom began to recognize the potential for something unique to come out of her guidance.

First, there was Chris, who was given a guitar as a gift after he had a hernia operation. In a way, it was intended to redirect his energies from jumping out of trees and off of buildings to a more passive hobby. It was a match made in heaven. Chris began to play and sing, and he got involved in a couple of musical groups with his school friends almost immediately. One of his first bands was called "The Native Cats."

Chris's musical prowess got Marian and Elaine interested in guitar too. It wasn't long before they discovered that their voices blended well together. Seeing the excitement that playing a guitar generated, I soon followed the trend, and in junior high school I began to play music with some of my friends, albeit a genre more tuned to Jimmy Hendrix and Led Zeppelin than folk music. Within no time, Phyllis was singing along with Marian, Elaine and Chris. I eventually was drawn into the group adding my rock styled guitar playing and singing.

The five of us were quite well musically integrated. Marian and Elaine had amazing abilities to pick out harmonies, and Phyllis could sing sweet and soft melodies. Chris had excellent melody and harmony abilities, and I was finding a comfortable spot supporting the bottom end singing bass. We learned to sing songs that were popular during the seventies. Famous groups like Crosby, Stills, Nash, and Young and the Beatles were just a couple of the bands that we loved to imitate. Our harmonies blended so well with each other that people often told us that we sounded just like the real thing. It was a magical combination!

Wanting to test our music on the local scene, we booked ourselves into a few local establishments. The reception at the clubs was always good. Even though we weren't even old enough to buy beer, aged eighteen to thirteen, they still allowed us to perform in their pubs. I think we had to be out by 9:00 pm.

We started to get invitations to perform in nursing homes and folk masses, and we sang anywhere else the doors would open to us. We were so naïve that we sang songs like *One Toke over the Line Sweet Jesus* and *Jesus Is Just Alright with Me* at folk masses because we thought they were spiritual songs. The priest used to look at us like we were from another planet, but he still accepted us. We would always follow those songs with something nice like *Blowing in the Wind,* thinking that was spiritual. With five parts of harmony, it drew lots of smiles, compliments, and forgiveness for the sixties styled, protest nature of the other songs. At least we saved *Puff the Magic Dragon* for the pubs!

One day, Mom decided it was time to test the strength of the group. She entered us into the Groton Naval Base talent show. There, we were officially named, The Bannon Family Singers. We dressed in a manner that showcased our connection as a family group and went out on stage belting out songs from Simon and Garfunkel to Peter, Paul, and, Mary. I can't help but laugh at the pictures of how we looked. It was somewhere between the Von Trapp Family and the Doobie Brothers with matching outfits and the girls wearing go-go boots. The raucous applause after each song was encouraging and when the show ended the trophies were brought out to be awarded to the top three competitors. We eagerly buzzed around the stage waiting for the results.

"Third place trophy goes to..."

"Second place trophy goes to…"

"And the first place trophy goes to… The Bannon Family Singers."

Mom was so excited and beamed with pride. The euphoric shouting from everywhere must have displaced her anxieties as to whether she was or wasn't doing a good job raising her six children. This was a testament to who she was and what she believed we could accomplish with patience and perseverance, which was something she knew about. She could now see the fruit of her years of teaching us those values taking hold. This apex of success and confirmation brought tears to her eyes.

Mom watched us perform with great pride as she thought back to what might have made her life very different. Had she actually followed the path of the scripts locked within her white pocketbook, all of this would never have happened. The day that Mom sat in her bedroom and faced a crossroad of paths having to decide between marrying her American hero or her Belgian admirer was now sealed in her mind as the day she made the right decision. This was worth every struggle she had endured after the war. Her legacy was cemented in history and she was happy to have followed that path..

Shortly after this euphoric experience, Mom faced a tragic event that would change the lives of the family forever. Elaine was driving Marian to visit their friends when, on a curvy road in Mystic, Connecticut, a drunk driver crossed the centerline and slammed her older Cadillac head-on into their Ford Falcon. This collision was anything but a fair fight of equals. Marian and Elaine both slammed into the windshield. The Falcon was destroyed but the driver of the Cadillac was able to walk away.

Elaine and Marian were barely alive when the ambulance arrived. They were given blood transfusions and taken to Lawrence and Memorial Hospital in New London. Marian had lacerations to her face that required hundreds of stitches. I remember going to see Marian in recovery a few days after the accident and being shocked at how her face had swelled like a basketball. This couldn't be Marian, I thought at first. Elaine had been scalped and required 200 stitches to reattach her hair. It had been peeled back and because it rested on her face, her hair could be saved. She recalls not being able to see after the crash because of her eyes being covered with her scalp. Elaine also injured one of her knees, and crushed her foot. This would put an end her skiing. It was one of her favorite hobbies.

The driver of the Cadillac was found to be at fault, but unfortunately, she had no insurance. There was little they could do to pay the hospital bills and replace the car. Eventually they found one small loophole that allowed one sister to sue the other for a seatbelt violation. They eventually collected a small settlement, and since the military ended up taking care of most of the hospital bills, Elaine and Marian used the leftover money to travel to France, Belgium, and England together.

It was risky sending two Americans girls over to Europe all by themselves. Elaine recalled that they broke a few hearts. One Englishman wanted to marry her and even sent her a letter in America. Mom intercepted the letter and never allowed Elaine's eyes to see the star-struck lad's missive. I don't think she wanted her daughter to end up in a transatlantic love affair similar to hers.

When Chris turned eighteen, he enlisted in the Army. In 1971, those who joined the army or were drafted were most likely to go to South Vietnam to fight against the Communist North Vietnamese. Chris's enlistment sent him to Army School, after which, the Vietnam War was nearing an end. His departure left a hole in the singing group, so Mike joined the band. He was learning to play bass guitar. With Mike's admittance the family group had five members again. The reorganized group didn't last long though. Shortly after Chris left, Marian signed up for the Army and was shipped off to Fort McClellan, Alabama. Phyllis met a gentleman and ended up moving to Minnesota. I was preparing to graduate vocational school soon, so I enlisted in the U.S. Army while I was still seventeen and finishing high school. I believe we all wanted to make Dad proud of us by following in his footsteps.

Eventually, most of us were scattered to different parts of the globe. Mike joined the Army when he turned eighteen and was sent to Germany. Marian also ended up in Germany near the end of her service. Just as I was leaving Germany to return home, she arrived for a year stay in a remote mountain village near the border of East Germany. I had not seen Marian for a long time, but we were able to connect for one day and talk about our family memories and our Belgian relatives. It was a tearful reunion that I hold very dear to my heart to this day. We had both just watched the emotional movie about another World War II survivor. The movie was called, *The Hiding Place*. We could see the similarities that our own family history had during the war. We wept as we hugged for a separation that would last another year.

Once the Bannon family children had finished their tours of duty, they all returned home to Noank. We knew it was never going to be the same as far as The Bannon Family Singers were concerned. Sure, we gathered together at special celebrations and took out the guitars for some fun group singing, but it wasn't the same. Mom would still sit there and smile as we sang. Aunt Grace would request her favorite song, *Country Roads,* by John Denver, and we would play and sing all of the oldies but goodies together. While

Mom hoped we would resurrect the family group, I think she also knew we needed to move on to pursue our own careers. At the dinner table, Mom sang to us her meal blessing that we always sang at our dinner table growing up. "Bene sen yu senior, Bene se serapa, serculion prepare, a circulon De Pan, a sis swatine." We never knew what it meant, but we always joined in.

We all still loved to sing and play music, but the family group was becoming a fond memory. It was clearly the highlight of my mother's years in America. She'd had many proud moments throughout our upbringing, but I think watching her children sing together was one of the top experiences in her life. From the music that she loved as a child but wasn't allowed to play during the occupation, to the music that Dad dazzled her with even though he was unable to read sheet music, then to the harmonious vocals that her children produced, music continued to be an important part of her life. It was fulfilling for her to feel as though she'd passed her love of music and her musical talents on to her children.

Occasionally, while living in Maine, Mom would sit at the piano and attempt to play, but it seemed that the music came very hard for her. Her memories of the joy of music did not fail, and she always managed to have the piano in her home wherever fate would place her. When Dad died in 1994, Mom insisted the piano follow her. The piano accompanied her from Connecticut to Maine during her yearlong stay. After all, it was the piano that first got the attention of Walter, the piano man, walking by the window when she practiced her Mozart in Bouillon. Mom was like the nightingale singing her lovely love songs to the ears of other birds flying by. The piano was the catalyst to her new life after the war. It was what began the process of what made everything in her life different.

For me, when I sat at the piano and played, it brought back memories of Dad playing it. Mom would sit next to me and listen intently. Though not an accomplished pianist, I have managed to play by ear like Dad used to do, and though she seemed a bit frustrated that I couldn't read music, she continued to applaud my every performance.

13. LESSONS LEARNED

As I near the end of this journey of recording her life, I have mixed feelings about my work. While I'm happy to have opened the vault of Mom's life for us to see the treasures inside, another part of me is sad to have opened that vault of her life that revealed the pain she endured.

Our house feels empty and oddly quiet now that Mom is living back in Connecticut. My dog misses her as well. He grew quite attached to her. While we were away at work every day, he would sit by her side and be her best friend. Mom would talk to Tanner in French all day long. I actually think he started to learn a second language.

She left here having taught me more than a few lessons. I guess a mother's job of teaching her kids really never ends.

Unexpectedly, I have been broken to the point of tears several times. This undertaking of writing her life experiences started out as a quest to find out what she lived through during World War II, but ended up doing so much more than giving me just an historical perspective. Writing this book has changed me. I never expected to be touched by the experience. My goal was to touch others with her story, but in the process of my research I discovered that similar pains fueled my own challenges.

Helping to organize her belongings led me through piles of notes, pictures, and letters. Some of these letters detailed her pain. Some letters justified her anger for being left alone to raise all six of us. Sometimes Mom cried alone, but we never knew about it. Sometimes Dad's attitude was cavalier, but we never knew about that either.

I think I understand her now a whole lot more than I did when she first moved into our home. I can see why she does what she does, why she acts like she acts, and why she says what she says. It's all about perspective. She looks at life differently than all of us, because she is looking down from a different mountaintop. I can look into her eyes now and understand that I am looking into the eyes of a woman whose eyes saw it all. The portrait of her that was painted by Albert Raty so long ago shows her looking away in the way I imagine she did when confronted by Nazi soldiers. Her eyes are tilted away just enough to avoid a confrontation, but not so far that she can't still see their every move. This was how she survived the war. At every challenge, she learned to make a calculated step, tiptoeing through the minefields. It was a very careful balancing act on a high wire of hope.

When Mom speaks I am careful to pay attention to every word that she says, because her voice is a voice of experience, being there, not reading about it or hearing about it. I get it now.

This week I called Mom to talk about her brother Pierre who had recently passed away. One of the first things she said to me was, "He survived the war with me." Then she paused as though pained too much to speak.

I said, "I know, Mom. I'm sorry."

I told her that she was the only surviving family member now, and she accepted that fact quietly, also without a response. I ended the conversation after telling her that. Her sadness only seemed to increase with my talking. I had hoped to encourage her with the thought that she, the daughter who was wrapped in the arms of love made by her father as they huddled together in the basement awaiting their final breath together, was the only remaining voice of their incredible plight. I reminded her that the story might have ended with her, but now, all because of that traumatic day when she fell down and broke her hip, all of us can take part in it.

I won't get upset if Mom ever tells me that she's not hungry, even if she hasn't eaten a meal yet on any particular day. I also know that I will never complain about food in front of her again. If these and the other lessons I learned having her live here would just stay branded in my mind, I would expect that I would never complain about anything again, no matter what.

I'll be cautious with people I meet, but I won't hold a relationship at bay, nor will I prejudge them because of their looks or heritage. Mom seems so friendly at times, that she is seemingly too trusting, but in an instant it can change and then she can seem to be somewhat cold. I discovered the reasons why. I hope I will always give everyone I meet the benefit of the doubt when it comes to first impressions.

Mom would give everything she owned to a person in need, without regard for herself. I know that Dad used to get upset with her for donating a portion of her small paycheck to support the church she attended. It reminds me of the story in the Bible where Jesus lectured some who contributed to the temple because in comparison to the poor woman who gave only a penny, which was all she had, they gave very little of their wealth.

I never knew Mom to hold back forgiveness, and yet I found out about the pain of un-forgiveness that she carried. Maybe I can learn to forgive others who've wronged me so that I don't carry that pain to my grave. I know the thought of forgiving Adolf Hitler is beyond what most of us will ever have to deal with, so it's difficult and unfair for me to try to compare her hurts with anything that I have ever experienced.

If I need to say I'm sorry to somebody, I should simply remember the huge task that Mom has in front of her and realize that my task is small and easily manageable in comparison.

Mom always drove me nuts whenever we were preparing to go somewhere. She would wake up two hours before it was time to go, and she would start to get ready. By one hour prior to our need to leave, she would be sitting in the chair with her coat on waiting for me. I would tell her that we still had plenty of time, but she just said that she is always ready. She said that when Dad was in the military, they always needed to be on time. I know that when she lived under occupation, they always needed to be ready to go in case of an emergency. I think this issue is a combination of the two experiences. I can understand that this habit was a routine of her life for twenty-seven years living with an army husband. Even though it would be okay for her to let the preparedness slip a bit, it is who she is, Miss Punctuality!

As I was preparing the last set of boxes to bring back to Mom in Connecticut, I was surprised again when I found a piece of paper in a notebook that had a headline reading, "Lessons Learned From War." Underneath that, were nine bold lines that read exactly this:

Survival. **Pray**

Don't complain

Help other people in need (Father ex)

Forgive

Do something good

Work hard

Plant good seeds

Do something for your country

God Bless America

Wow, this was interesting. I had to consider how this list, that she made long ago, lined up so well with everything I had been writing about her over the last two years. While I thought I understood her life, I now had a validation of her character. It was the perfect time for me to find this note that summarized her philosophy.

I've heard some people say that time heals all wounds. I know this is not necessarily true. I heard another point of view that says time just helps you to forget the details. I know Andree has not forgotten all of the details. I wish that I could get a filmstrip of what her eyes saw and play it on a wall for others to watch. I'm sure they would all be impacted as I have been.

Almost every chance she gets now, Mom sits at the shore off of Noank Beach or Stonington Point and looks out across the ocean towards Europe. I don't know what she's thinking. Maybe she ponders what life may have been like had she married that other Belgian gentleman. I can only guess, but I'm certain that she misses Bouillon.

The wounds of war for her will never be forgotten nor will they ever completely heal. For those of us who've never lived it, may we learn from those who have, in hopes of avoiding a repeat of this terrible tragedy. Perhaps we'll be fortunate enough never to see war like Mom did. War is never pretty. World War II is said to have been the most brutal and violent war in all of history. To think that the world powers were all colliding just seventy years ago is difficult for us to imagine. I know that there are fewer and fewer lucky ones alive today to tell of their experiences. Thankfully, her's has been captured. I realize now that we were all fortunate to have Mom spend time in Maine, living with us for over a year. I told her on that painful day that she sat in the hospital in North Conway that we needed to look for the good that can come out of difficult times. I know now that we both found that good.

Mom didn't know that she would touch my life this way, but such is her *motus operandi* now. Her list said it on line number five, "Do something good!"

She certainly did that with her presence in our home.

14. CLOSING THE POCKETBOOK

It's winter of 2012 in Mystic and Mom has settled into a rental. When I visited her we talked about the book project. First she asked why it was being called *The White Pocketbook*, so I reminded her of how she told me the story of her white pocketbook when she was young. She had shared how she had lost the pocketbook during the war, and then told us about having it returned after the war. She smiled and said, "Oh yes."

I then read some of the chapters of the book to her, and she sat there nodding in agreement. Once in a while she would interject a small fact that I hadn't known about. I wrote everything down and entered them into the manuscript's pages when I returned to Maine. When I read the section to her about her having to live in her basement during the war she said, "That's why I will never live in a basement again." I can understand this now, but I never knew it was an absolute requirement to her accommodations.

Another statement she made when we were discussing the castle in Bouillon was, "I was in love with Godfroi." Then she reached into her pocketbook and handed me a picture of her hugging his statue. I asked her if I could make a copy of the picture and she said okay, but she wanted it returned quickly to be placed safely back into her pocketbook.

From where I was sitting, my entire perspective had been changed. I should have had this book to read when I was ten years old, and again when I was sixteen, and then again when I was twenty-one years old. I think it would have given me a much better understanding of her life and mine. Unfortunately, her story remained small fragmented vignettes until now. I'd heard bits and pieces of her experiences, but without the details we now have, I simply didn't equate her life to that of others who've recorded their remarkable war experiences and have shared them with the world.

We are fortunate that Mom kept everything. At the beginning, I was frustrated that she had stored so many papers. She had my first grade report card, and my friend's school pictures from kindergarten through to sixth grade.

She had pictures I had made and letters I had written. She had my high school running stories and pictures of my team. She had my life history! Multiply this times six and you can visualize how many boxes she had stored. I often got angry about how one person could have had so many boxes of things to transport along her life's journey, but now I am glad that she did this. Every piece of paper, whether torn or whole, seemed to add support to everything I've written about her in this book.

Because of her compulsive hoarding, no longer will this one voice be relegated to the lists of names and faces in the shadows. Now, from the quiet life of a once young Belgian girl, a loud cry is heard and her story is told.

One Sunday during a visit to Connecticut, we had a chance to visit my oldest sister Marian and her husband John. Elaine, Chris and I sat with her and sang one of our old favorites, *One Toke Over the Line Sweet Jesus* and a few other of her favorite songs from earlier times. She seemed to enjoy them as a single teardrop fell from her eyes. She kept a tight hold of Chris's hand during the entire visit. When I left, she grabbed mine and held it tight. I know she remembered these songs that meant so much to us growing up.

We finished our trip to Mystic taking Mom out to dinner with eighteen other family members. This included her children, her grandchildren, and her great grandchildren. During the meal Mom looked at me and said, "I still eat like the war."

I said, "Yes, Mom, I see that." Then I looked across to my wife who has been with me through almost every part of this experience. I wondered if she'd heard what Mom had just said. She then acknowledged it with a nod and, once again, it confirmed everything I had recently learned.

I asked Mom if she would sing to us the French dinner blessing, which of course, she did with pride. Those of us who remembered it tried to join in, "Bene sein you Senoir Bene se sera pa a sir culoin de pan a sis swatine."

Before leaving Connecticut, I needed to make one last stop to some fond places of my youth. The school was first. Sadly, it was closed down. The roof didn't look so tall now that I'm not so small. I wanted to climb the building just to see what the view looked like now with all those new homes standing where the woods used to be, but I'm not as nimble as I used to be. I also didn't need to get into any trouble on this visit.

I then went to the playground and saw the telephone pole that I used to climb. It would be even easier now because there was a little maple tree growing along side of it.

After seeing the telephone pole, I drove to the home that was our proving ground for twenty years. I could still see the places Dad used to practice shooting his rifles. Pretty much every inch of the old yard spoke to me about a childhood memory.

Finally, I drove to the shore at the town dock to look out towards Fishers Island. "Wow, it's a long way to that island," I said to the gentleman there on the beach. He nodded and smiled in agreement almost as if to wonder what planet I was from.

I snapped a few pictures and as I headed back to my car, the horn of a distant boat echoed out. I turned to look again at the beautiful scene one last time.

The memories of my youth are still vivid. Time has not erased the good or bad ones. In fact, for me, time has made me long for more visits to the land of my youth. I can't help but think this is what Mom ponders when she stands at the water's edge and looks towards Europe. While it's not likely she would ever go there at this point in her life, she can always travel there in her dreams.

Her pocketbook will be mailed back to her soon, and she can browse the pictures and notes. In her heart, she can escape back to those days of climbing the castle walls, picking flowers, and dreaming of heroes and knights and of who her hero might be. I will sneak in one new note to the contents of her purse however. It will read…

Dear Mom, You have been my pillar of strength and statue of pride. I thank you for never giving up. You always made a way to survive those difficult times. I'm proud to have a mother like you. You were and still are fearless like Godfroi De Bouillon. His spirit lives in all of us now, thanks to you. You are my hero. Love, Walter

Andree's first communion

Walter & Andree

Walter & Andree's growing family

The beach in Lapanne and early motorcycles

Elizabeth & Andree

Bannon Family & one unknown extra

Bannon Family Singers

Marian, Mike, Elaine, Walt

The home in Noank

Works Cited

Levi, Primo. Inside Anne Frank's House. Westra. New York: Overlook Press, 2004 "Godfroi De Bouillon King of Jerusalem" http://encyclopedia2.thefreedictionary.com . 2012. 26 Apr. 2012Douffet, Michele. "Albert Raty, 1889-1970 Synopsis", 2009. 26 Mar. 2012. http://www.tandem-productions.beKristallnacht . www.ushmm.org/museum (United States Holocaust Museum) Washington, DC. 26 Apr. 2012Degrelle , Leon. The Story of the Waffen SS, Hastings: Castle Hill Publishers, 1984Roosevelt, Eleanor. The Autobiography of Eleanor Roosevelt, New York: HarperCollins, 1961Emerson, Ralph Waldo. www.famousquotesabout.com/quote/To-be-yourself-in/469604 2012. 26 Apr. 2012"76,000 civilians lost in Belgium" http://en.wikipedia.org/wiki/World_War_II_casualties 2012. 26 Apr. 2012Degrelle, Leon. The story of the Waffen SS. By Leon Degrelle. Hastings: Castle Hill Publishers, 1984"Only regrets", "That we lost the war" http://www.germandaggers.info. January2005. 28 Apr. 2012"Soldiers died in Battle of the Bulge" http://en.wikipedia.org/wiki/Battle_of_the_Bulge. 26 Apr. 2012"Church in Suer de me killing of innocents", massacres of WWII http://www.scrapbookpages.com/Oradour-sur-Glane/index.html 1998. 26 Apr. 2012Dobson, James. The Only cure for Bitterness, Dr. James Dobson's Bulletin: May 1999

ABOUT THE AUTHOR

Walt Bannon lives in Maine with his wife Marilea. His first book, Digger Down, is a comical adventure about his bottle collecting hobby. This book however is a serious non-fiction work that employs the same touching style that made his first book so enjoyable. Some creative literary liberties were taken to make the book a complete work but all his writings contained herein are from actual life experiences.